The

Ultimate Unofficial

Chicago Cubs

Puzzles & Trivia

The Ultimate Unofficial Chicago Cubs Puzzles & Trivia
Copyright © 2011 by SJJ Inc.

ISBN 978-0-9828792-0-7

Illustrations: Robert Jackson
Layout: MaryKay Hruskocy Scott

Printed in the United States of America.
10 9 8 7 6 5 4 3 2 1

Distributed by:
Cardinal Publishers Group
2402 N. Shadeland Ave., Suite A
Indianapolis, IN 46219
(317) 352-8200
www.cardinalpub.com

Wrigley Field bleachers.

Suntan lotion on my neck.

A Cubs day game. Yea!

— S.J. Jiminez (2010)

Table of Contents

Albert Spalding

Chapter 1

History

The official beginning of the Chicago Cubs franchise was 1876 with the formation of the eight-team National League. Financed by William Hulbert and led by pitcher/manager Albert Spalding and infielders Ross Barnes and Cap Anson, the Chicago "White Stockings" won the league's first championship.

Following Hulbert's death in 1882, the recently retired Spalding assumed ownership of the team and Chicago won its third consecutive NL pennant under player/manager Anson. Chicago won three more pennants under Anson before he was relieved of his duties as a player and manager prior to the 1898 season.

The name "Cubs" was first used in 1901, but didn't take hold until 1907. In the early years, the franchise was referred to as the White Stockings, Whites, Silk Stockings, Black Stockings, Colts, Orphans, Rainmakers, Rough Riders, Panamas, Microbes, Zephyrs, Nationals and Spuds.

Chicago dominated the NL in the early 1900s, winning four league titles and two World Series from 1906-10. William Wrigley Jr. became a minority owner of the Cubs in 1916 and soon became the majority owner. The Cubs continued to enjoy success on the field and at the box office. They won the NL pennant in 1918, '29, '32, '35, '38 and '45, but did not win a World Series.

The Wrigley family owned the Cubs until 1981 when the Tribune Co. took control. The Cubs won the NL East Division in 1984, '89, 2003, '07 and '08, and qualified for the postseason as the Wild Card team in 1998. The team's only series win was the 2003 NL Division Series.

The Ricketts Family bought the Cubs in 2009.

Cubby Holes

Fill in the missing letter for each of the words listed. Be careful, because all of the words can be completed with more than one letter. Transfer the correct letter to the corresponding line so that the result is a two-word term from the early days of Chicago's National League team. Solution on page 135.

___	___	___	___	___		___	___	___	___	___	___	___	___	___
1	2	3	4	5		6	7	8	9	10	11	12	13	14

1. CRO __
2. __ ITS
3. LIV __ D
4. __ IGHT
5. SHAR __
6. LO __ E
7. S __ RAP
8. B __ TH
9. __ ASE
10. TA __ E
11. R __ NG
12. TOR __
13. STA __ E
14. BIN __

Strike Three

From this list of six words, determine which three words have what the other three don't have. Answer on page 135.

ICEBERG

ISOTOPE

RELIANT

SHACKLES

SLEEPY

STINKER

Su-Mac-Ku

Use logic to fill in the grid below so that every row, every column and every 3 x 3 box contains the letters M-C-G-L-O-T-H-E-N, in honor of Lynn McGlothen, a Cubs pitcher from 1978-81, who was tragically killed in a fire at the age of 34. Solution on page 135.

C			T		H			M
		E				G		
M	N						O	T
		M		O		C		
	H		L		N		T	
		T		C		H		
E	O						N	C
		L				E		
T			E		O			L

```
                J
              D R E
            S T U A N
          E H C O R M K
        D N S A H N O I I
      R E N E U R E E C R N
    E I M G A M O T F T H E S
    T C P R G M O H N F N E Z
    I K S E O O E D K E I O R
    H E T B R R L L U C T N F
    W T E D Z W O O G K I T G
    T T R N E I C N C G U R H
    B S S A L L K A A R I F B
      L I S A L M I R E D R
        U E N I A R A D S
          E N A N O Y K
            Y M R S N
              S S A
                B
```

Cubs Conundrum

Find items in the categories listed, going up, down, sideways or diagonally in the puzzle grid on page 10. No letter will be used more than once. When you have found all 21 items, there should be 11 unused letters. Starting at the top of the grid and going across each row, spell out a hidden word with those unused lettters. Hint: the word is another name for "Cubs." Solution on page 136.

6 Cubs on the 2010 Team

_____

_____

_____

_____

_____

_____

5 Cubs in the Hall of Fame

_____

_____

_____

_____

4 Cubs Managers

_____

_____

_____

_____

3 Cubs Colors

_____

_____

_____

2 Former Cubs Announcers

_____

_____

1 Cubs Ownership Family

_____

Hidden Word: _____

History Crossword
Solution on page 135.

Across

1. Bullpen aces
8. Rub elbows with
14. "Gabby"
16. 2nd largest city in Illinois
17. Person that is evaluated
18. Pull toward with a fake bunt (2 wds.)
19. Pronoun in a Hemingway title
20. Chicago's st.
22. Player publicity, slangily
23. Possess
25. There are usually nine in a game
29. "___ show time!"
32. Used to be
33. Indian bread
34. Make known
36. Nag
39. O'Hare flight data, briefly
40. Boot a ground ball
41. Bluenose
43. Liquor
46. Concession stand french fries veggie
48. Baseball know-it-all
49. Rookie's nickname, often
50. Figure out
51. Dulled
54. Sheryl Crow lyrics: "...no one said ___ be this hard..."
55. Sprinted to second base
56. Wind up?
58. Yankees' Ruth
62. Chicago's NHL foe
66. Unleavened
69. Dugout bellyacher
70. "Ryno"
71. "You ___ bother!"
72. Transition

Down

1. Player's plug of tobacco
2. Mascara site
3. Approximately (2 wds.)
4. Flower stalk
5. USNA grad
6. i-___ monitor
7. Bud holders?
8. Ate a hot dog at the game
9. Lord's Prayer starter
10. Victoria's Secret item
11. A season without a victory
12. Rocket gasket
13. "Mr. Cub"
15. ___ Aviv
21. Sharply hit baseball
23. Be in the red
24. Coach: "My ___ or the highway!"
26. A Bobbsey twin
27. Catch a few Zs before the game
28. Bumbling
29. Treatment for a player's sprained ankle
30. Young Cubs fans
31. Football center's responsibility
35. Hand gesture for victory
36. Mins. and mins.
37. Rugged rock

38. Sky box?
40. Musical exercise
42. Fielder's cry: "I've ___ it!"
44. Same old, same old
45. Anger
46. Barbecue site
47. Peculiar
49. Abduct
51. "Three Finger"
52. Bat shaper
53. Score a go-ahead run
57. Some fraternity men

58. Baby's napkins
59. Offshore
60. Cubs right-handed pitcher who made his MLB debut in 2009, Justin ___
61. Barely beat
63. In addition
64. Cyst
65. OF Shamsky or P Ceccarelli
67. Genetic letters
68. Cubs commercials

Andre Dawson

History Trivia
Answers on page 136.

1. Name two of the three Cubs who played in both the 1984 and '88 National League Championship Series.

2. Which team did the Cubs beat in the National League Division Series in 2003, their first postseason series win since 1908?

3. Jim Hendry was named the Cubs General Manager in 2002. Who was the club's President/CEO that he replaced?

4. Which American League team swept the Cubs in the 1938 World Series?

5. How many games in a row did the Cubs win in 1935 en route to the National League pennant?

6. Who was the San Francisco Seals outfielder the Cubs decided not to pick up their option on in 1934 who went on to a Hall of Fame career?

7. Why did the Cubs and Boston Red Sox players threaten a strike in the midst of the 1918 World Series?

8. Which Red Sox pitcher won two games in that Series, then went on to make a bigger name for himself as a hitter?

9. True or False? The entire Chicago team was arrested in the third inning of a game.

10. The club's only Around the World Tour of 1888-89 included stops in eight foreign countries (plus Hawaii). Name two of the countries where Chicago played.

11. Match each player with his more colorful nickname:

Mordecai Brown	Bull
Forrest Burgess	Dizzy
Jay Dean	Gabby
William Dillhoefer	Goose
Leon Durham	Hippo
Richard Gossage	Peanuts
Charles Hartnett	Pickles
Harry Lowrey	Rabbit
Walter Maranville	Smoky
James Vaughn	Three Finger

12. Which team won the only All-Windy City World Series in 1906?

13. In the Cubs miserable collapse in 1969, what was the largest lead in the standings the team had in mid-August?

14. Which Cubs relief pitcher gave up a walk-off home run to the San Diego Padres' Steve Garvey in Game 4 of the 1984 National League Championship Series?

15. Who was the Cubs first baseman who made a critical error in the deciding Game 5 of that Series to give the Padres a 6-3 win and deny the Cubs a trip to the World Series?

16. Who is the only player in Major League history with three seasons of 60 or more home runs?

17. What were the first products the Wrigley Company sold when it was created in 1891?

18. Which of the Tribune Company's stations was televising Cubs games when the company bought the team in 1981?

19. How did the Ricketts family attain its wealth?

20. Who was the Cubs infielder who died of cancer at the age of 27 in 1981?

21. Where did the Cubs (and White Sox) hold spring training during the World War II years (1943-45)?

22. Who was the Cubs starting pitcher in Game 7 of the 1945 World Series who gave up five runs in the first inning without getting anyone out in the 9-3 loss to the Detroit Tigers?

23. From 1922 through 1947, the Cubs had a Hack on their roster. Match each Hack with his tenure with the Cubs:

Stan Hack	1922-25
Hack Miller	1926-31
Hack Wilson	1932-47

24. Which U.S. President did the Cubs team visit in the White House during the 1888 season?

25. Which Cubs pitcher is tied with Christy Mathewson for the National League record for victories in a career?

Su-Hen-Dree-Ku

Use logic to fill in the boxes so every row, column and 2 x 3 box contains the letters H-E-N-D-R-Y, in honor of Jim Hendry who was named the Cubs General Manager in 2002. Solution on page 137.

N					R
			H		
Y		R	N		
		N	D		Y
		H			
E					N

History
Mini-Crossword
Solution on page 137.

Across

1. Gym unit
4. Little League coach, often
7. Center of teammate?
8. Big bird at Brookfield Zoo
9. Sash for Japanese baseball fan
10. Coal container
11. Before, in poetry
12. Thrust to catch a line drive
14. Cubs curse subject (2 wds.)
16. Contradict
17. Bloop single's path
18. Win by one run
19. Top pitcher
20. Recipe amt.
21. Tell a whopper
22. Reserved
23. Illinois driver's lic. and others

Down

1. Sets your position in the outfield again
2. Aggrandize
3. Greek letter
4. Remove errors from
5. Body builder? (2 wds.)
6. Denims
11. "Chicago" lyricist
12. Homophone of 21-Across
13. List abbr.
15. Like Leo Durocher
19. Rhyming boxing champ

After solving the crossword puzzle, use the letters in the grid to answer the additional clue. Transfer the letters in numbered boxes to the corresponding blanks below. (Or answer the additional clue first to help you solve the crossword puzzle.)

Equipment with 108 double stitches, weighing 5 to 5 1/2 ounces.

___ ___ ___ ___ ___ ___ ___ ___
16　5　22　2　14　19　21　12

Ernie Banks

Chapter 2

All-Stars

The first Major League Baseball All-Star Game was the brainchild of Chicago Tribune sports editor Arch Ward. It was played in 1933 at Chicago's Comiskey Park as part of the city's "Century of Progress" World's Fair. The Cubs were represented in that first game by shortstop Woody English, catcher Gabby Hartnett and pitcher Lon Warneke.

The Cubs have had 87 players named to the National League team since the Midsummer Classic began. Ernie Banks holds the distinction of appearing in the most All-Star Games as a Cubs player. He was chosen to play in 14 classics. Ryne Sandberg was selected to the NL squad 10 times, Ron Santo nine times, Billy Herman seven times and Sammy Sosa seven times.

The only Cubs manager to manage in an All-Star Game (2003) was Dusty Baker.

Marlon Byrd was the lone Cubs player selected to the 2010 NL squad. It was a memorable night for the centerfielder who was playing right field in the ninth inning. Byrd made a bit of history, recording the first outfield force out in an All-Star Game in 53 years. He caught on one hop what appeared to be a pop single, then fired the ball to second base to force runner David Ortiz, helping preserve the National League's 3-1 win. Byrd scored the NL's third run in the seventh inning, racing home from first on a bases loaded double into the right field corner. "I saw it coming off the bat," Byrd said of the bases clearing hit, "and started running like I stole something."

Wrigley Field has played host to the All-Star Game three times: 1947, 1962 and 1990.

What's in a Name?

An anagram is a word, phrase or sentence formed by rearranging all the letters of another word, phrase or sentence. For example, an anagram for the name of Cubs pitcher LEE SMITH is THE SMILE. Rearrange the letters of these anagrams to come up with the first and last names of Cubs All-Star players.

1. SEND NO AWARD   _____

2. RING ONE'S DESK   _____

3. KEEN BRAINS   _____

4. AM KIND VEGAN   _____

5. DAVID'S JOY   _____

6. TEAM NERDS PRY   _____

7. IRK PRO ARM   _____

8. A SASSY MOM   _____

9. COLD LAB MILK   _____

10. ENERGY BRANDS   _____

Now it's your turn. See if you can create anagrams for these Cubs All-Stars that fit their baseball persona. Our answers are on page 137, but there are no right or wrong answers.

11. LEON DURHAM (think young power hitter)

12. BRUCE SUTTER (think about what a relief pitcher is, quite often)

Su-Do-Curt

Use logic to fill in the grid below so that every row, every column and every 3 x 3 box contains the letters C-U-R-T-D-A-V-I-S, in honor of Curt Davis, a Cubs All-Star pitcher in 1936. Solution on page 138.

I		D						A
	V		R				U	
				T				I
			V		T		I	
		R				C		
	T		D		S			
T				S				
	U				C		D	
C						T		R

Su-Do-Kiki

Use logic to fill in the boxes so every row, column and 2 x 3 box contains the letters C-U-Y-L-E-R, in honor of Hall of Fame outfielder Kiki Cuyler, an All-Star with the Cubs in 1934. Solution on page 138.

		U			L
		R		E	
U			R		C
R		Y			E
	R		E		
Y			L		

All-Stars' Mini-Crossword

Solution on page 138.

Across

1. Cubs C who was an All-Star in 1984 & '86
6. Players' work organization
7. Saying "Strike three!" again
11. Has nachos in the stands
12. Way, way off, like Dodger Stadium
13. One of the letters on a Giants cap
14. To and ___
15. "___ play two today!"
17. Urgent request to an umpire
18. Most error-filled game
20. Less common than most records
21. Cubs P who was an All-Star in 1994 & '95

Down

1. Windy condition on the infield that causes a delay (2 wds.)
2. Ballpark picnic pests
3. By way of
4. Itty-bitty bit
5. Fans with congested noses
7. Highlight film units
8. Stand for a portrait
9. Nostrils
10. Cubs foe who was an 8-time All-Star SS and NL MVP in 1960
16. Neuter
17. Chicago's Navy ___
19. Opening for season or game

After solving the crossword puzzle, use the letters in the grid to answer the additional clue. Transfer the letters in numbered boxes to the corresponding blanks below. (Or answer the additional clue first to help you solve the crossword puzzle.)

Cubs' five-time All-Star pitcher in the 1940s.

___ ___ ___ ___ ___ ___ ___
17 2 18 5 11 12 6

Apt Description

Fill in the blanks to complete an apt description of a Cubs
All-Star. Place the letters you use to complete the words onto the
corresponding line to form the name of the All-Star player.
Answer on page 137.

"M __ .   C U __ "   W A S   T H __   __ I C __ N A M E
   2   6   1   8   9

G __ V E __   T O   A   H __ L L   O F   F A M __
 4   3   7   5

S H O R T __ T O P .
         10

___ ___ ___ ___ ___   ___ ___ ___ ___ ___
 1   2   3   4   5   6   7   8   9 10

All-Stars' Trivia
Answers on page 138.

1. How did the Cubs acquire Ernie Banks?

2. Which Cubs Hall of Fame second baseman holds the Major
League record with five hits on Opening Day?

3. Who was the Cubs' 47-year-old relief pitcher in 1970 who
was the first Major League hurler to appear in 1,000 games?

4. Since 1960, only three right handed hitters have won more than one National League batting title. Roberto Clemente and Tommy Davis are two of them. Who is the third?

5. Which Chicago Hall of Fame pitcher became the long-time owner of the Washington Nationals/Senators?

6. Match each player with the college he attended:

Mark Grace	Arizona State University
Ken Holtzman	San Diego State University
Dave Kingman	University of Illinois
Rick Monday	University of Southern California
Rick Reuschel	Western Illinois University

7. What disease caused the amputation of both of Ron Santo's legs?

8. Who was player-manager of the Cubs' 1938 team that won the National League pennant?

9. Who did the Cubs send to the Philadelphia Phillies to acquire Ryne Sandberg (and Larry Bowa)?

10. Which Cubs All-Star outfielder was the first player to hit two home runs in a game off Sandy Koufax?

11. Who was the native Chicagoan, and later a Cubs player, who is the youngest player to appear in a World Series game?

12. Which Hall of Fame second baseman, and a member of the Cubs' 1938 World Series team, was a member of the New York Yankees' famed "Murderers' Row?"

13. Which Cubs first baseman was called by baseball historian Bill James as "the worst player in the Hall of Fame?"

14. Besides Barry Bonds and Willie Mays, which Cubs Hall of Fame outfielder is the only player with 400+ home runs and 300+ stolen bases in his career?

15. Which Hall of Famer is the only Cubs player to lead the National League in stolen bases three consecutive seasons?

16. Who was the Hall of Fame outfielder the Cubs lost to the New York Mets in the expansion draft of 1962? Hint: He went on to a career as a long-time broadcaster with the Philadelphia Phillies.

17. Name the Hall of Fame Cubs player mentioned in Ogden Nash's "Line-up For Yesterday" poem that appeared in *SPORT* magazine in 1949:
    B is for ___
    Back of the plate;
    The Cubs were his love,
    and McGraw his hate.

18. Which Cubs All-Star infielder returned to his alma mater, the University of Mississippi, in 1991 as head coach of the school's baseball team?

19. Which Cubs Hall of Fame pitcher played basketball in the off-season with the Harlem Globetrotters?

20. Who was the Hall of Fame Cubs pitcher in the 1930s who was the last player to be allowed to throw a legal spitball in a Major League game?

21. Which team did these Cubs stars play their last Major League game with?

    Ferguson Jenkins   Ron Santo   Billy Williams
    Greg Maddux   Sammy Sosa

22. Baseball Commissioner Kenesaw Mountain Landis prevented the Cubs' Hack Wilson (coming off his record-breaking 1930 season) and the White Sox's Art Shires from doing what?

23. In 1944, which Cubs All-Star outfielder was given an intentional walk with the bases loaded?

24. Who was known as "The Mayor of Wrigley Field?"

25. In the 2003 Hall of Fame vote, Cubs closer Lee Smith was eligible for the first time. He finished with 42 percent of the vote (well short of the necessary 75 percent for induction) and finished seventh in the balloting. Three former Cubs players were among those ahead of him. Who were they?

Pick-Off Play

Pick one letter in each pair of letters to spell out the last names of these Cubs All-Star players. For example, BC AE HN KP MS is BANKS. Answers on page 139.

1. BI TU CD KN MN EI RS   _____

2. DM AU DT BD EU XY   _____

3. HS EO RT MN AE NT   _____

4. PT AR EL LM ES IL NR OS   _____

5. AW LO OO DT   _____

6. MS TW IO SO HL EO RT   _____

7. BN ER CD KL AE RS ST   _____

8. DR EU LN PS TV EO NY   _____

9. HL AI CW KN MS AO EN   _____

10. CG AR AY CT ES   _____

All-Stars' Crossword
Solution on page 140.

Across

1. Salad green
6. 11-time All-Star who is known as "Mr. Cub"
11. Team equipment man's piercing tool
14. Turned on the lights at Wrigley Field (2 wds.)
15. Brookfield Zoo heavyweight that is a big fan of Sandberg?
16. Aloha Grill necklace
17. Sharp
18. Like some cereals
19. Chicago's st.
20. Cubs' "Athletic Director" from 1963-65, Col. Robert ___
22. Jetty
24. Santa's helper
25. Fancy clothing
26. ___ Ridge, Ill.
29. Craze
32. Ballpark fig.?
33. Back then
34. Like hitting for the cycle
36. Enjoy an ice cream cone in the bleachers
40. "Woe is me!"
42. Get the fans pumped (2 wds.)
43. Toy that has its ups and downs
44. Group that sang "Take Me Out to the Ball Game" at Wrigley Field: *N ___
45. Salute the crowd
46. Chinese principle
47. Stadium bustle
49. Dick Durbin's pos.
51. Musty, like the dark parts of Wrigley Field
52. Branchiate

55. Lab eggs
57. Chicago, Burlington and Quincy rails foundation
59. Exceptional ability
63. Barley bristle
64. Grammarian's concern
66. Speck in the ocean
67. Opposing team's scoundrel
68. Runs out of gas on the mound
69. Like rich infield soil
70. Navy Pier rank (Abbr.)
71. 9-time All-Star third baseman who hit 300+ career home runs
72. Hall of fame?

Down

1. Cat's scratcher
2. Loaded, like Tom Ricketts
3. Needle holder
4. 6-time All-Star who relied on his split-finger fastball
5. Curse of the Billy Goat, e.g.
6. Forehead
7. Triumphant cry
8. Tiny complaints
9. As high as the patella
10. Sub finders
11. Assumed name for a player
12. Cubs pitcher, Randy ___
13. 2-time All-Star pitcher who joined the Cubs in 2007
21. Wide of the plate
23. Damply
26. Sheep cries
27. Hideous looking win
28. WGN-TV sports director, Dan ___
30. Wrigley Field suite carpet layer's calculation

31. 2-time All-Star catcher who managed a Canadian Baseball League championship team
35. Umpire's regulation
37. Smidgen
38. Shade of blue
39. Oddball player
41. Burn in the locker room shower with hot water
42. Zimbabwe, formerly
48. First games for rookies
50. Hide-hair link
51. 8-time All-Star who was NL MVP in 1987
52. 3-time All-Star first baseman who won a World Series with Arizona
53. From Cap Anson's home state
54. Hits the runway with the team plane
56. Magician's cry
58. "Shucks!"
59. Alfonso Soriano's home currency
60. Starlin Castro's distinctive flair
61. NCAA Final Four game
62. Player's eyelid problem
65. Understand

Fergie Jenkins

Chapter 3

Pitchers

The only 200-win pitcher in Cubs history was Charlie Root, who compiled a record of 201-156 from 1926-41. His 16 years in a Cubs uniform is tops for pitchers. Root's best season was 1927 when he won 26 games and had 145 strike outs, both career highs.

The most memorable Cubs pitcher, though, is Ferguson Jenkins. In 10 seasons (1966-73 and 1982-83), "Fergie" had a club record 2,038 strike outs while winning 167 games. He was named the NL's Cy Young Award winner in 1971 when he went 24-13 with a 2.77 earned run average.

Hall of Famer Bruce Sutter ranks as one of the top relief pitchers in history. In five years in Chicago, he had 133 saves, 32 wins and 494 strike outs in 493 innings. He won the Cy Young Award in 1979.

Other Cubs pitchers to win the Cy Young were Rick Sutcliffe in 1984 (going 16-1 after the Cubs acquired him in a mid-season trade) and Greg Maddux in 1992 (20-11 with a 2.18 ERA).

The top pitcher on the Cubs' World Series championship teams was Mordecai "Three Finger" Brown. He won 186 games for the Cubs from 1904-12 (and had two more wins in 1916), compiling an ERA of 1.80. In 1906 he had a 26-6 record with a 1.04 ERA.

Other pitchers in the Baseball Hall of Fame who played with the Cubs include: Goose Gossage (1988), Dennis Eckersley (1984-86), Hoyt Wilhelm (1970), Robin Roberts (1966), Dizzy Dean (1938-41), Burleigh Grimes (1932-33), Grover Cleveland Alexander (1918-26), Rube Waddell (1901) and John Clarkson (1884-87).

Su-Moe-Ku

Use logic to fill in the boxes so every row, column and
3 x 3 box contains the letters of a memorable Cubs player (who
"is still considered the best pitcher that Ozanna, Poland, ever
produced"). When completed, the row indicated by the arrow will
spell out the name correctly. Solution on page 140.

		K		S	R	O		
R	A				D			
W			O			A		
		Y	S				W	O
O	W				K	R		
		B			S			D
			K				B	S
		W	R	B		K		

Square Pitchers

Each square contains the 8-letter name of a Cubs pitcher. The name
can be found by beginning at one of the letters and reading either
clockwise or counterclockwise. Answers on page 140.

1. L E S
   T   H
   R A C

2. C O L
   A   L
   S T I

3. U E R
   S   L
   C H E

4. A N H
   M   O
   Z T L

5. S K I
   W   B
   O R O

6. U B E
   R   T
   D E T

Alphabet Soup

Use all 26 letters of the alphabet to complete the names of seven Cubs pitchers. Each letter will be used just once, and only one letter is to be used per dash. Solution on page 140.

A   B   C   D   E   F   G   H   I   J   K   L   M

N   O   P   Q   R   S   T   U   V   W   X   Y   Z

1. ___ U E ___ E D O

2. ___ A M ___ R ___ N O

3. ___ E N ___ ___ N ___

4. ___ I ___ ___ O ___

5. ___ A ___ ___ S W ___ R T ___

6. ___ O ___ N ___

7. ___ E ___ ___ S ___ ___ R

Su-Bon-Ku

Use logic to fill in the boxes so every row, column and 2 x 3 box contains the letters B-O-N-H-A-M, in honor of Bill Bonham who won 53 games for the Cubs from 1971-77. Solution on page 141.

		H	N		
N	A			B	
				M	N
O	M				
	N			A	O
		M	B		

Build the Name

Use the letter groups—one at the beginning and one at the end—to build the names of Cubs pitchers. Each letter group will be used just once. Answers on page 141.

ELL	ER	FFE	GO	HEL	JE	MA	NS
ON	OW	RE	RTH	SU	SUT	TI	UX

1. _____ CLI _____

2. _____ DD _____

3. _____ TT _____

4. _____ NKI _____

5. _____ RD _____

6. _____ DR _____

7. _____ USC _____

8. _____ SWO _____

Keeping Up With the Joneses

The Cubs have had four pitchers with the surname of Jones. But there have been five pitching Smiths and four pitching Johnsons, Millers and Williamses. From these lists of first names, determine which match each surname. Answers on page 141.

Surnames: JOHNSON, JONES, MILLER, SMITH, WILLIAMS
First Names:

1. Doug	2. Abe	3. Brian	4. Bob	5. Bob
Percy	Ben	Jerome	Charlie	Kurt
Sam	Bill	Mitch	Dave	Ox
Sheldon	Ken	Pop	Lee	Wade

Pitchers' Word Search

Find the Cubs pitchers' names in the letter grid. The names run up, down, sideways and diagonally. Some of the names overlap. Solution on page 141.

```
F  G  O  R  D  O  N  I  K  R  A  L  S  C  D
L  L  A  R  E  V  O  K  I  S  H  S  M  S  O
J  E  N  K  I  N  S  B  C  O  R  U  I  P  O
L  H  T  R  O  W  S  L  L  E  E  T  T  A  W
W  C  W  O  R  D  I  T  D  Y  B  T  H  L  J
X  S  A  O  V  H  Z  N  O  R  O  E  S  D  J
D  U  B  T  E  M  A  A  E  W  R  R  U  I  G
P  E  E  N  A  X  C  U  Z  O  O  E  R  N  K
F  R  R  N  E  T  L  D  X  H  W  T  O  G  Q
I  Y  N  L  W  B  B  R  A  T  S  S  U  R  B
E  N  A  H  A  L  L  A  C  N  K  P  L  E  R
S  U  T  C  L  I  F  F  E  R  I  M  I  M  O
T  N  H  G  U  A  V  V  A  K  X  E  L  I  W
E  M  Y  E  R  S  A  L  G  U  O  D  L  E  N
R  S  F  D  M  C  C  A  L  L  I  Q  Y  W  Q
```

ABERNATHY	DOUGLAS	LILLY	RUSH
ALEXANDER	ELLSWORTH	MCCALL	SMITH
BECK	GORDON	MCDANIEL	SPALDING
BOROWSKI	HENRY	MYERS	SUTCLIFFE
BROWN	HOLTZMAN	OVERALL	SUTTER
BRUSSTAR	HOWRY	PFIESTER	TIDROW
CALLAHAN	JENKINS	REULBACH	VAUGHN
CLARKSON	LARKIN	REUSCHEL	WEIMER
DEMPSTER	LEE	ROOT	WOOD

Pitchers' Mini-Crossword

Solution on page 141.

Across

1. That girl
4. St. Louis player, briefly
8. Dissenting vote
9. Mixed bag
10. Ticket sellers' place
12. No game today
13. Player's swelled head
14. Pitcher nicknamed "The Red Baron" (Cubs 1984-91)
18. Training table caviar
19. Indian bread
20. Ant crushers
23. There are six per inning
24. CIA predecessor
25. Thai currency
26. Tire pressure unit: Abbr.

Down

1. Mix-up in the box office
2. Misrepresentation
3. Batter's asset
4. Short Welsh dog
5. Standoffishness
6. Jacksonville Jaguars coach, Jack Del ___
7. A DiMaggio brother
10. Call for help
11. Tennis champ, Monica ___
15. West ___ swing
16. Iran language
17. Great Lakes Naval Training Station rank: Abbr.
20. Cry loudly after a loss
21. Sine ___ non
22. Bounce of the ball

After solving the crossword puzzle, use the letters in the grid to answer the additional clue. Transfer the letters in numbered boxes to the corresponding blanks below. (Or answer the additional clue first to help you solve the crossword puzzle.)

All-Star pitcher in 1940 who had 95 wins and 21 shutouts in seven seasons with the Cubs.

___ ___ ___ ___ ___ ___
16 18   3 19   4 22

Pitchers' Trivia

Answers on page 142.

1. Who did the Cubs obtain in June 1984 in a trade with the Cleveland Indians who went 16-1 the rest of the season en route to winning the Cy Young Award?

2. In 1988, who was the first Cubs pitcher since 1909 to throw a shutout in his Major League debut?

3. Which Cubs pitcher played for Venezuela in the 2006 and '09 World Baseball Classics?

4. Which Cubs pitcher was the first African-American to throw a no-hitter in the Major Leagues?

5. Which former Cubs pitcher is the only person to play in and be an umpire in a Major League All-Star Game?

6. Who was the future Hall of Fame pitcher the Cubs acquired from the Pittsburgh Pirates in exchange for a cigar?

7. Who were the first brothers in Major League history to combine for a shutout?

8. Name the two Cubs pitchers who won "Pitching's Triple Crown" (leading the league in a season in Wins, Strike Outs and Earned Run Average).

9. Which Cubs pitcher was called to active duty by the Illinois National Guard during the riotous 1968 Democratic National Convention in Chicago?

10. Which two future Hall of Fame pitchers did the Cubs acquire in 1966?

11. Cubs great Ferguson Jenkins was born in Canada. Which other Cubs All-Star pitcher is from Canada?

12. Who was the relief pitcher the Cubs traded in 1983 who went on to become the American League Most Valuable Player for the Detroit Tigers in 1984?

13. Which Cubs pitcher hit a home run on the first pitch of his first Major League at bat in 1992?

14. The only Cubs pitcher with three no-hitters was Larry Corcoran (from 1880-84). Who is the Cubs pitcher with two?

15. Name the two Cubs pitchers who threw no-hitters in 1972.

16. Who was the pitcher the Cubs selected in the first round of the first Major League Baseball draft in 1965?

17. Who were the two pitchers the Cubs received from the St. Louis Cardinals in the Lou Brock trade?

18. Which Cubs pitcher went 0-for-1962 at the plate to set a Major League record for worst batting average in a season?

19. Why was Mordecai Brown called "Three Finger?"

20. Who was the Cubs pitcher in the only nine-inning double no-hitter in Major League history?

21. Which former Cubs hurler, who was elected to the Hall of Fame, gave up Kirk Gibson's memorable walk-off home run in the 1989 World Series?

22. Who are the only two Cubs pitchers to win the Reliever of the Year award?

23. Which Cubs pitcher tied a Major League record (now with 51 other pitchers) by striking out four batters in one inning in 1974?

24. Which Cubs pitcher won the National League Rookie of the Year award in 1998?

25. Which player pitched for more Major League teams (12) than anyone else? Hint: He played for the Cubs from 1992-95 and again in '98.

Pitchers' Round

Identify the Cubs pitchers described in the eight clues, then place the six-letter names of the pitchers in the corresponding section of the concentric circles on the next page. The first letter of each name should be placed in the shaded circle and the remaining letters placed in the circles going toward the ball in the center. When you have successfully identified all the pitchers, the name of the Cubs' first pitching superstar will be revealed in the outermost circle, starting at 1 and reading clockwise. Hint: His name was tossed around every Major League ballpark on a daily basis for more than a century after his playing days were over. Solution on page 142.

1. 1979 NL Cy Young Award winner.

2. Rookie in 2009 who was 3-1 in 20 relief appearances.

3. Cubs' Minor League Pitcher of the Year in 2008 who made his Major League debut in 2009.

4. Had a perfect game in the World Series; played his final MLB game as a Cub in 1967.

5. Winning pitcher in the Cubs' first night game at Wrigley Field.

6. Left-handed pitcher for the Cubs in 1994; now is a pitching coach in the Cardinals' organization.

7. Began his 22-year MLB career with the Cubs in 1967; won 221 games (97 fewer than his brother).

8. Had a no-hitter for 8 2/3 innings in his Cubs debut in 1993.

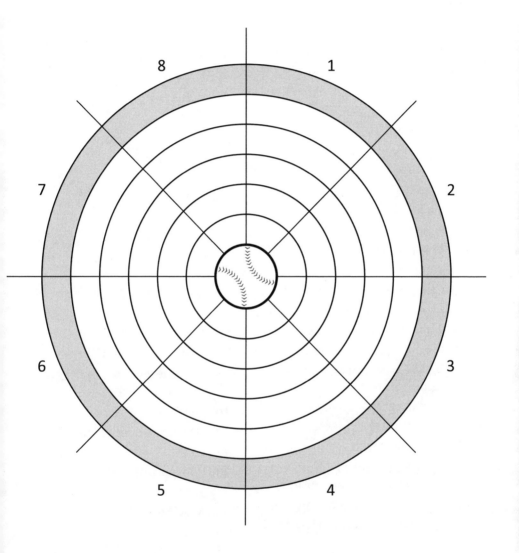

Pitchers' Crossword
Solution on page 143.

Across

1. Cultural values
6. Besides Bob Feller, only MLB pitcher to strike out their age in a single game
10. Cubs pitcher, ___ Pisciotta
14. Nutso
15. Continental currency
16. Finished
17. Cubs' 2005 draft pick and SS prospect, ___ Johnston
18. Drops a pop fly
19. Indian home (Var.)
20. Former Bulls GM and coach
22. Arabic for peace
24. Woodworker's tool
26. Consider as a god
29. Knot the score again
30. 9-inning contest
32. Give up
33. Had 53 saves in 1993, an NL record
34. Baltimore Orioles color
36. Aquatic plant
38. Stretches dough
40. Highfalutin
44. High school draft pick, usually
46. Bulls' Central Division rival
48. All-Star in 1983 and '87 as a Cubs closer
52. Jump for a line drive
54. Give off, as light
55. Button material
56. Recluse
58. Take care of the tickets cost
59. Turkish capital
61. Face-to-face exams
63. Surprise attack
64. Central points
67. Game under the lights, slangily
70. Patella's place
71. Soon, to a bard
72. "Silly" birds
73. HR: Go ___
74. Cubs' career victory leader
75. Mongolian abodes

Down

1. Antiquity, once
2. Cracker Jack bonus
3. Only pitcher to throw two no-hitters for the Cubs
4. Brilliantly colored fish
5. Church council
6. Ballpark hot dog
7. "Days of ___ Lives"
8. Bruins legend, Bobby ___
9. Pushover
10. Rock band ___ Crue
11. Fly a plane over Wrigley Field
12. Fix
13. Criminal offenses
21. Withdraw
23. Naval unit
24. In times past
25. Cubs 3B in 1958-59, he managed five teams in the Major Leagues from 1961-77
27. Kind of approval
28. Scream at the umpire
31. WSW opposite

35. Assemble
37. A line drive between outfielders
39. Hawk tickets
41. Coke chiller
42. Cubs' All-Star pitcher in 2008
43. Lyric Opera of Chicago highlight
45. "The Matrix" role
47. Hog's home
48. Crotchety
49. Jose's tomorrow

50. Lousier
51. Dealt to another team
53. Consecrate
57. Slender and long-limbed
60. Way, way off
62. In ___ of (replacing)
65. Lennon's lady
66. Dove's sound
68. Citi Field winter hrs.
69. Hi-___ graphics

Gabby Hartnett

Chapter 4

Catchers

Charles "Gabby" Hartnett was one of the greatest field/hit combination catchers in MLB history. He became the first catcher to top 30 home runs, 100 RBI and a .300 batting average in a season with 37 HR, 122 RBI and a .339 average in 1930. Hartnett was the National League Most Valuable Player in 1935 when he hit .344 with 32 home runs and 91 RBI. He was a six-time All-Star and was elected to the Hall of Fame in 1955.

But his most memorable moment was in 1938: the so-called "Homer in the Gloamin.'" The Cubs were battling the Pittsburgh Pirates for the NL lead and were tied with the Pirates in a late-September game. With two outs in the bottom of the ninth and the umpires ready to call the game due to darkness, Hartnett hit an 0-2 pitch into the bleachers. That put the Cubs into first place en route to the NL title.

Randy Hundley (1966-73 and 1976-77) set a Major League record for catchers by appearing in 160 games in 1968 and caught 150 or more games in three consecutive seasons, also a MLB record. He won a Gold Glove in 1967 and was an All-Star in 1969.

Other top catchers for the Cubs were Roger Bresnahan (1900, 1913-15) who is a member of the Baseball Hall of Fame, Johnny Kling (1900-11) who caught more than 1,000 games and helped the Cubs win four NL titles, Steve Swisher (1974-77) an All-Star in 1976, Jody Davis (1981-88) who had seven hits, six RBI and a .389 batting average in the five-game 1984 NL Championship Series, Joe Girardi (1989-92, 2000-02) an All-Star in 2000 and Geovany Soto (2005-2010) who was the Rookie of the Year and an All-Star in 2008.

Cryptic Quote

The Cryptic Quote is a substitution cipher in which one letter stands for another. If you think that A equals Z, it will equal Z throughout the puzzle. Solve the Cryptic Quote to find a Cubs catcher's saying, along with the player's name. Answer on page 143.

"F D M   B D K B J Z U   B L E I   J T M   R K Y M   T L I D

I F T M M F — J   R U F   U A   I K X Z R M I,   E L F   X U

J B F K U X."

—Q U M   Z J T J Z K U R J

Next-Door Neighbor

Replace each letter with the letter that comes directly before or after it in the alphabet to form the names of Cubs catchers. For example, you would replace M with either L or N. Answers on page 143.

1. R P S N
2. G V M E M F X
3. E B U H T
4. V J M J J M R
5. F H S B S E H
6. T D S U B H T
7. R X J T G F S
8. G B Q S O D S U

Catchers' Mini-Crossword

Solution on page 143.

Across

1. Catcher who also has played for the Dodgers and Diamondbacks (Cubs 2007-10)
5. Starting C in Game 7 of 1987 World Series with Cardinals (Cubs 1983-86, 1993)
9. Team promoter's creative spark
10. Norse war god
11. Chic
12. Refer to
13. Pause between bases
15. Butterfly catcher
16. Showy flower
21. Achievement on the field
22. Pitcher ___ Hershiser
23. A single time
24. It may be out on a limb
25. Caught Tom Browning's perfect game with the Reds in '88 (Cubs 1999-2000)
26. 2008 NL Rookie of the Year (Cubs 2005-10)

Down

1. A pitch above the letters
2. Inactive
3. Grasslands
4. Covered in plastic, like a press pass
5. Sites
6. Mine entrance
7. 1992 US Open golf champ, Tom ___
8. WSW opposite
14. C Pawelek or P Abernathy
16. C Oliver or OF Hiser
17. Cleats' shoestring
18. Black-and-white cookie
19. "___ we forget"
20. Anthem chorus member
21. In favor of

After solving the crossword puzzle, use the letters in the grid to answer the additional clue. Transfer the letters in numbered boxes to the corresponding blanks below. (Or answer the additional clue first to help you solve the crossword puzzle.)

Cubs catcher from 1979-81 who had eight RBI in one game.

___ ___ ___ ___ ___
21 10 18 14 8

Name Grid

These Cubs catchers' names are listed in alphabetical order according to length. Fit them into their proper places in the grid on the next page. We've started your solving by placing the name MILLER (make certain you scratch it off the list). Now look for a 10-letter name that begins with M. Continue working that way until you've filled in the grid. But be careful. There might be a name that seems to work in more than one place, but each name is used just once. Solution is on page 144.

4 Letters
DALY
OWEN
SOTO
TODD

5 Letters
CHITI
DAVIS
FLINT
FOOTE
KLING
MCVEY
WHITE

6 Letters
ATWELL
MILLER
NEEMAN
TAYLOR
WILSON

7 Letters
BARRETT
BERTELL
BURGESS
GIRARDI
THACKER
SERVAIS
SWISHER
WILKINS

8 Letters
HARBIDGE
HARTNETT
SANTIAGO
WILLIAMS

9 Letters
BERRYHILL
BRESNAHAN
KITTRIDGE
SCHEFFING

10 Letters
CANNIZZARO
LIVINGSTON
MCCULLOUGH

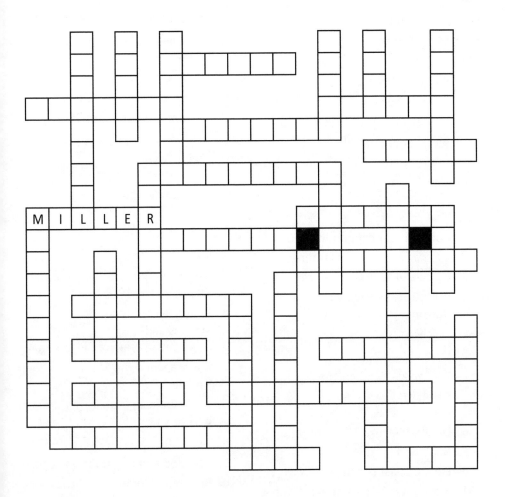

Catchers' Crossword

Solution on page 144.

Across

1. Cheap Cubs tickets: ___ song (2 wds.)
5. Succeed on the mound (2 wds.)
10. Jewish month before Nisan
14. Mine entrance
15. Get used (to)
16. Actress Spelling
17. Canceled as the starting pitcher
18. Leases a place in Wrigleyville
19. Big galoots in White Sox gear
20. Italian brandy
22. Stop running
23. Chills and fever
24. Unit of work
26. Cubs All-Star catcher in 1976
28. Illinois State Capitol feature
32. C Pawelek or P Lilly
33. Awestruck at seeing the Cubs in person
34. Chicago's st.
36. Prohibits
41. Breakfast, lunch and dinner
43. Floral necklace
45. Ear-related
46. Diminutive, like Mike Fontenot
48. Bat wood
50. Pacific Coast League city
51. Start of an Arizona cheer: Gimme ___! (2 wds.)
53. Road trip baggage
55. Cubs All-Star catcher in 1951
59. WSW opposite
60. 1954 NL Rookie of the year, Wally ___

61. Video game: "Call of Duty: Black ___"
63. Expose
68. Boston Celtics great, Larry ___
69. Ward off
71. Kosuke Fukudome's home continent
72. "If all ___ fails..."
73. Bear trap
74. "Rambling Wreck From Georgia ___"
75. Deli breads
76. Test format
77. First family's home

Down

1. Canine tooth
2. Skunk's defense
3. Capital of Latvia
4. Sitting in roof-top seats at Wrigley Field
5. Cubs All-Star catcher in 2000 who has managed the Marlins and Yankees
6. Lance Johnson's uniform number
7. Part of UNCF
8. Team illustrator
9. Mended a ripped uniform seam
10. Book needed for a road trip
11. Player's moolah
12. Bicker with an ump
13. Escalating fastball, briefly
21. Relief pitchers' area, for short
25. Chutzpah
27. Promotions director's concept

28. Alternative to steps at Wrigley Field
29. S-shaped molding
30. One way of fitting (3 wds.)
31. Wrinkly fruit
35. Grassy area
37. Small town
38. Artificial turf layer's calculation
39. Gave the bullpen a buzz
40. Ballpark cocktail: ___ gin fizz
42. Cubs headliner
44. ___ of Capri
47. Sign a bonus check

49. Cubs All-Star catcher in 1969
52. Colorado trees
54. "Holy cow!"
55. Glowing remnant
56. End table linen
57. Not as good
58. South American range
62. Locker room hot tubs
64. Diminish
65. Brought into play
66. "Good catch!"
67. "The Boys of Summer" author
70. Pitcher's stat

Catchers' Trivia

Answers on page 145.

1. In 1993, which Cubs player became just the seventh catcher in Major League history with 30 or more home runs and a .300+ batting average in a season?

2. How many games did Randy Hundley catch in 1968 to set a Major League record? Bonus points for naming any of the other five players to catch for the Cubs that season.

3. Who was the player-coach who caught 26 games in 1962?

4. Which former Cubs catcher was co-host of the *Today Show* on NBC from 1969-73?

5. Which Cubs catcher hit a home run in his first Major League at bat on Sept. 1, 1961, and then never hit another one?

6. Which Cubs catcher played for Team USA in the 2006 World Baseball Classic?

7. Who was named the National League's Rookie of the Month for April 2008?

8. What country is Geovany Soto from?

9. Who was the then-minor league catcher the Cubs received (along with pitcher Steve Stone) from the Chicago White Sox in exchange for Ron Santo?

10. Name one of the three catchers who played in the 1998 postseason for the Cubs.

11. Besides Todd Hundley, which other Cubs catcher in the 21st century was the son of a former Big League catcher?

12. Whose catcher's mask was one of the first artifacts acquired by the Baseball Hall of Fame?

13. Which Cubs catcher was selected by the Colorado Rockies in the expansion draft, then wound up winning a World Series as manager of the New York Yankees?

14. Which Cubs player was the first rookie catcher to start on the National League All-Star team?

15. Who was the Cubs catcher dubbed "Hank White" by the team's TV announcers?

16. Which Cubs catcher, who was named to the 1976 National League All-Star team, has a son playing in the Big Leagues?

17. Which sport did Cubs catcher Johnny Kling win a world title in while sitting out the 1909 season because of a contract dispute?

18. Randy Hundley won a Gold Glove in 1967. Who is the only other Cubs catcher to win the award?

19. Which Cubs catcher severed his fingers with a table saw, had them reattached, then returned to the line-up months later?

20. Cubs catcher Pop Shriver made news in 1894 by being the first person to catch a baseball dropped from more than 500 feet from what?

21. Which Cubs catcher tripled, then stole home in a 1966 game?

22. Which Cubs catcher made an obscene gesture to Wrigley Field fans while rounding the bases after hitting a home run in a 2002 game?

23. Who was the Cubs catcher in 2003 who was not allowed to join the MLB players union (and share in certain League revenues) because he was a replacement player during the 1994 strike?

24. Which Cubs catcher was the only one to hit for the cycle (a single, double, triple and home run in one game)? Hint: He did it less than a month after Billy Williams hit for the cycle, too.

25. Which Cubs catcher was banned from international competition for two years after testing positive for marijuana use at the 2009 World Baseball Classic?

Su-Gas-Ku

Use logic to fill in the grid below so that every row, every column and every 3 x 3 box contains the letters G-A-S-T-F-I-E-L-D, in honor of catcher Ed Gastfield, who was 0-for-3 with three passed balls in his only game in a Cubs uniform in 1885. Solution on page 145.

I			A			D		
I				A				D
			T		G			
		F		E		S		
	T						A	
A		D				I		F
	L						E	
		T		I		E		
			D		F			
G				L				T

Ron Santo

Chapter 5

Infielders

Tinker to Evers to Chance. It's one of the most famous lines in baseball history and it refers to the Cubs infielders who won four National League pennants and back-to-back World Series titles in 1907 and '08.

Shortstop Joe Tinker (1902-12, 1916) played 1,536 games with the Cubs, hitting .259 with 304 stolen bases. Second baseman Johnny Evers (1902-13) played 1,409 games, batting .276 with 291 stolen bases. First baseman Frank Chance (1898-1912) played 1,274 games, batting .297 with a club record 400 stolen bases and 590 RBI.

Ernie Banks (1953-1971) was the NL MVP in 1958 and '59. The shortstop/first baseman had 512 HR and 1,636 RBI in 2,528 games. Said teammate Ron Santo: "If Ernie Banks had played in the 1990s, with the media exposure we have now, he would have been Michael Jordan."

Third baseman Bill Madlock (1974-76) won back-to-back NL batting titles in 1975 and '76 and his Cubs career average of .336 is No. 2 on the team's all-time list. Second baseman Rogers Hornsby (1929-32) holds the club's modern-day season records for batting average (.380 in 1929) and runs scored (156 in '29). Hall of Fame second baseman Billy Herman (1931-41) played 1,344 games with the Cubs, hitting .309. His 57 doubles in 1935 and '36 are still tops for a Cubs player in a season.

Second baseman Ryne Sandberg (1982-94, '96-97) was a 10-time NL All-Star, the 1984 NL MVP, the 1990 NL HR leader, a nine-time Gold Glove winner and was elected to the Hall of Fame in 2005. Hall of Fame first baseman Cap Anson (1876-97) holds team career records for hits (3,055), runs (1,719) and RBI (1,879).

Chicago Cubes

Read the clues and fill in the appropriate boxes. The answer to the second clue is the answer to the first clue, plus one letter. The answer to the third clue is the answer to the second clue, plus one letter. And so on. (The order of the letters may change.) Solution on page 146.

1. Letter on Oakland's cap
2. "Away" on a team's schedule
3. Rode the pine
4. BASEBALL: LINE-UP as THEATRE: _____
5. Dugout wear for pitchers, usually
6. Cubs' rookie shortstop in 2010

Double Play

The names of two players who played the same position have been combined on each line. The letters of each name are in the correct order, but you need to break apart the names to come up with the Cubs infielders. Answers on page 146.

1B BLUCEKNEER

2B BASANKEDBERRG

3B RACMIEREZY

SS DUTHENSRITOONT

1B DUGRHRAACEM

2B BETRICKERLLOT

3B SAMANDLOTOCK

SS KEBSASINNKGERS

Across and Down Words

There are 10 baseball terms and a Cubs phrase in the diagram. Taking one letter from each box across the top row, find a 4-letter baseball term. Cross off the letters as you use them. Do the same for the other five rows. Then take one of the remaining letters from each box and go down the first column to find a 6-letter baseball term. Cross off those letters. Do the same for the other three columns. The remaining letters, one per box, will reveal the phrase, reading left to right, row by row. Solution on page 146.

Across

_____

_____

_____

_____

_____

_____

B		A		B		L	
C	D	H	U	L	U	S	S
B		A		I		E	
O	T	H	I	M	S	I	R
D		B		A		L	
F	U	O	T	P	U	N	S
B		I		A		G	
E	M	M	T	I	T	N	T
G		A		M		E	
L	R	E	O	N	R	L	S
A		N		E		E	
B	E	R	U	N	T	O	T

Down

_____

_____

_____

_____

Phrase

_____

All Mixed Up

Unscramble the last names of these Cubs infielders. Answers on page 146.

1. AAACERRTTV _____

2. AEHMNR _____

3. BHNORSY _____

4. EIKNRT _____

5. EERSV _____

6. ACCEHN _____

7. AEGLNOZZ _____

8. BCEEEHLLU _____

9. HNNOORTT _____

10. DEEJSSU _____

Su-Bon-Kura

Use logic to fill in the boxes so every row, column and 2 x 3 box contains the letters B-O-N-U-R-A, in honor of Zeke Bonura, a Cubs first baseman in 1940 who is better known as being the youngest male athlete to win an event at the National Track Championships. He was a javelin throwing phenom at age 16. Solution on page 146.

	O		N		
			O	U	
A		N	U		O
B		O	R		A
	A	R			
		U		R	

Infielders' Trivia
Answers on page 146.

1. Who was the Cubs Opening Day starter at third base in 1991 and '92?

2. Which Cubs infielder hit home runs from both sides of the plate in two games in 2002?

3. Who was the Cubs second baseman and the National League's Rookie of the Year in 1962, who died in an airplane crash in 1964 after getting his pilot's license two weeks earlier?

4. Which Cubs player was the first African-American to start at shortstop on a regular basis in the Major Leagues?

5. Who was the first African-American on the Cubs' roster?

6. Who did the Cubs select with the first overall pick in the 1982 Major League draft? He became the first position player selected by the Cubs in the draft since it began (in 1965) to represent the team in an All-Star Game.

7. Which Cubs infielder was the first player to hit a home run for Team USA in the World Baseball Classic?

8. Who was the Cubs shortstop from 1948-53 whose son played shortstop in the Big Leagues from 1975-87?

9. Which Hall of Fame first baseman hit three of his 534 career home runs with the Cubs?

10. Who am I?
    I attended Lane Tech High School, 14 blocks from Wrigley Field.
    I hit a home run on the first pitch in my first Major League start.
    I was the National League's Most Valuable Player in 1945.

11. Which Cubs shortstop had the only unassisted triple play in club history?

12. Which Cubs infielder was given the Hank Aaron Award in 2008 as the most outstanding offensive performer in the National League?

13. Who was the Cubs third baseman on the 1908 World Series championship team who was later banned from baseball for allegedly attempting to fix games?

14. Who are the only two Cubs shortstops to win a Gold Glove?

15. Which former Cubs first baseman was shot in Chicago's Edgewater Beach Hotel by an obsessed teen-age girl in 1949?

16. Which *Phil Silvers Show* character was named after a Cubs first baseman?

17. Which Cubs third baseman, the son of a Major League pitcher, played in the 1988 All-Star Game?

18. Who was the first baseman who was a member of the Cleveland Indians when the game began, but hit a 14th inning walk-off grand slam to beat the Montreal Expos on Aug. 8, 1980?

19. Which two Cubs were teammates on Louisiana State University's NCAA championship baseball team in 2000?

20. Which Cubs second baseman played 123 consecutive games without an error, a Major League record (since broken)?

21. Ryne Sandberg won a Gold Glove and led the National League in runs scored three different seasons, but which Cubs second baseman accomplished that feat first, in 1968?

22. Which Cubs second baseman scored more runs in one season in the 20th century than any other right handed hitter in the National League?

23. Which Cubs first baseman played with the Boston Celtics in the National Basketball Association and had a critically acclaimed role in the TV mini-series *Roots*?

24. Who was the flamboyant Cubs first baseman from 1970-73 who owned a bar on Division Street, after playing in two World Series with the New York Yankees?

25. Which Cubs third baseman (who hit a home run in consecutive pinch-hit at bats) played trumpet with the Central Michigan University marching band at halftime of two Chicago Bears games at Wrigley Field, then went on to play in Johnny Carson's *Tonight Show* band?

Su-Wil-Ku

Use logic to fill in the grid below so that every row, every column and every 3 x 3 box contains the letters W-I-L-K-E-R-S-O-N, in honor of Curtis Wilkerson, who played second base, shortstop and third base for the Cubs in 1989-90. Solution on page 147.

	S					O	I	
	L						K	E
I		K	R			N		
N				S		O		
			W		L			
		I		R				S
		R			K	L		I
	K	O					S	
		E	N				W	

Infielders' Mini-Crossword

Solution on page 146.

Across

1. Third baseman known as "The Penguin" (Cubs 1983-86)
4. Grazing area
7. Egg cells
8. Win big
10. Church bench
11. Addiction
12. "Gesundheit!" receiver
14. "___ we there yet?"
15. Northwestern University frat letter
19. Muse of poetry
20. Game ticket listing
22. Uneasy feeling late in the game
23. Had a hot dog and pretzel
24. Batting cage prop
25. First baseman traded to the Braves (Cubs 2004-10)

Down

1. Uniformed stadium security
2. Nights before big games
3. Sign of boredom with the game action
4. Garage job
5. Arab ruler
6. Well-chosen
8. Second baseman traded to the Dodgers (Cubs 2005-10)
9. Player's eye color
13. Bridge seats
15. Sea eagle
16. Leaf in a game program
17. Word-of-mouth
18. Written reminder
19. Dine at Harry Caray's Tavern
21. Pee-___ League

After solving the crossword puzzle, use the letters in the grid to answer the additional clue. Transfer the letters in numbered boxes to the corresponding blanks below. (Or answer the additional clue first to help you solve the crossword puzzle.)

Nine-time Cubs All-Star third baseman.

___ ___ ___ ___ ___
12 6 18 24 7

Billy Williams

Chapter 6

Outfielders

Sammy Sosa hit a team-record 545 home runs for the Cubs from 1992-2004, including 66 in 1998. He had 425 total bases in 2001, 160 RBI in '01 and a .737 slugging percentage in '01. Staggering numbers. But years from now, will Sosa be in the Hall of Fame or a forgotten man, hidden behind MLB's asterisks?

Another Cubs outfielder left little doubt about his Hall of Fame status. Hack Wilson (1926-31) averaged 128 RBI and 32 HR a year for Chicago. His 1930 season was one of the greatest: .356 batting average, 56 HR and 191 RBI (a MLB record that still stands).

Andre Dawson (1987-92) was elected to the Hall of Fame in 2010. His six seasons in Chicago were highlighted by 49 HR, 137 RBI and the MVP award in '87, two Gold Gloves and five All-Star Game appearances.

Other Cubs outfielders in the Hall of Fame include King Kelly (1880-86), Hugh Duffy (1888-89), Kiki Cuyler (1928-35), Chuck Klein (1934-36), Freddie Lindstrom (1935), Ralph Kiner (1953-54), Monte Irvin (1956), Richie Ashburn (1960-61), Lou Brock (1961-64), whose one claim to fame in a Cubs uniform was hitting a home run over the center field fence in the Polo Grounds, and Billy Williams (1959-74), who averaged 25 HR, 25 doubles, 85 RBI and a .296 batting average over his career.

Also deserving mention are Hank Sauer (1949-55) who was the NL MVP in 1952, Bill Nicholson (1939-48) who was a four-time All-Star and led the NL in HR twice, Cy Williams (1912-17) who led the NL in HR in 1916, and Wildfire Schulte (1904-16) who helped the Cubs win four pennants while leading the league in HR twice.

Outfielders' Mini-Crossword

Solution on page 148.

Across

1. Left-handed pitcher turned outfielder (Cubs 1968-70)
6. Team bean counter, for short
9. "Let's play two ___"
10. Chicago's infamous ___market Square
11. High gear in a car
13. Shade of green
14. Pennant ___
15. Outfielder Cubs selected in the 1st round of the 1986 draft (Cubs 1990-94)
16. Locker room cold cuts, e.g.
18. Tit for ___
21. Type of fly or bunt
23. Bat wood
24. Illustrious
25. First baseman in a comedy skit
26. Outfielder who was the Phillies' hitting coach in 2010 (Cubs 1977-78)

Down

1. Addison station, e.g.
2. Relocate to another team
3. Manager's brainstorm
4. Bat goo: pine ___
5. Drinking lots of water before a game
6. Fashionable
7. Surface a stadium parking lot
8. Affirmative vote
12. Cubs pitcher, ___ Burris
15. Spring training mo.
16. Beat to a pulp
17. Stadium sound effect
18. Jackson 5 member
19. No. 1 pitchers
20. OF Savage and P Lilly
21. Wood-cutting tool
22. 3-___-4 at the plate

After solving the crossword puzzle, use the letters in the grid to answer the additional clue. Transfer the letters in numbered boxes to the corresponding blanks below. (Or answer the additional clue first to help you solve the crossword puzzle.)

Cubs outfielder in 1984-85 who had a record seven consecutive hits in the 1990 World Series with the Reds.

___ ___ ___ ___ ___ ___ ___
5   8   18   6   5   17   14

Su-Daw-Son-Ku

Use logic to fill in the boxes so every row, column and 2 x 3 box contains the letters D-A-W-S-O-N, in honor of Cubs outfielder Andre Dawson. Solution on page 148.

	W				
		S	D		
		W	S		D
O		D	W		
		O	A		
				W	

Double Switch

The first and last names of 10 Cubs outfielders have been split into two-letter segments. The letters in each segment are in order, but the segments have been mixed up. Put together the pieces in each line to come up with the players' names. Answers on page 148.

1. ES AL IS OU MO _____

2. GA TT WS HE MA RY _____

3. AY ND MO CK RI _____

4. SE JO RD CA AL EN _____

5. GE GE AN TM AL OR _____

6. WI LS ON CK HA _____

7. CU KI YL KI ER _____

8. RO CK UB LO _____

9. RL ON MA RD BY _____

10. IN LE KK UC CH _____

Cubs TXT

Use your cell phone keypad to help decode these Cubs outfielders' last names. In the example 2973, the 2 could be A, B or C; the 9 could be W, X, Y or Z; the 7 could be P, Q, R or S; and the 3 could be D, E or F. The player's name found in that text is B-Y-R-D, Marlon Byrd, the Cubs' center fielder. Now try these. Answers on page 148.

1. 94554267

2. 329766

3. 74455477

4. 7674266

5. 6239

6. 72356

Outfielders, From A to Z

Use the listed letters to fill in the blanks to complete the last names of these Cubs outfielders, from A to Z. Solution on page 148.

A __ __ __ A __   LMNT

B __ __ __ __   NORW

C __ __ __   RUZ

D __ __ __ __ __   ANOSW

E __ __ __ __ __ __   DDMNOS

F __ __ __   DLU

G __ __ __ __ __ __   DINOOW

H __ __ __ __ __ __   ACIKMN

I __ __ I __   NRV

J __ __ __ __ __ __   ACKNOS

K __ __ __ __ __ __   AGIMNN

L __ __ __ __ __   ANOTW

M __ __ __ __ __ __ __   AEINRTZ

N __ __ __ __   HORT

O ' __ __ __ __ __   AELRY

P __ __ __ __ __ __ __ __   AENORSTT

Q __ __ __ __ __   ALLSU

R __ __ __ __ __   DEHOS

S __ __ __ __   HIMT

T __ __ __ __ __ __ __   HMNOOPS

U __ __ __ __   EHRS

V __ __ __ __ __   AHORS

W __ __ __ __   DOOS

__ __ X   FO

Y __ __ __ __   GNOU

Z __ __ __ __ __ __ __   AABMNOR

73

Outfielders' Crossword
Solution on page 149.

Across
1. Part of Wrigley Field covered with ivy
5. Mike Perez, as a collegian
10. Abner Doubleday's military academy alma mater
14. Locale, like Wrigleyville
15. Pueblo brick
16. Four-star review
17. Dusty Baker's team after the Cubs
18. Long tresses
19. Little devils
20. Cubs outfielder in photo (2 wds.)
23. Pitcher's stat
26. Used to be
27. 11-Down mate
28. Guy's date to a game
31. Left field line at Wrigley: 355 feet or 108.2 ___
33. Jersey arm
35. A run
36. Track markings
37. Grazing area
38. Ron Santo's uniform number
39. Mario's Butcher Shop offerings
41. "Take your hands off me!" (2 wds.)
43. Pluses
45. More spine-tingling
46. Giant Hall-of-Famer, Mel ___
47. Barely win, with "out"
49. Team CEO's degree, often
50. Coconuts Music stacks
51. Featured player's uniform number

54. All-Stars Carty or Petrocelli
57. Engine supercharger
58. Bleacher wood, usually
62. Player's on-line journal
63. Clubhouse floorboard sound
64. Worshipped player
65. Former Cubs pitcher Vito Valentinetti's New Rochelle campus
66. Pays attention to a coach
67. Substance found in a bat of the featured player

Down
1. Combat
2. "___ we having fun yet?"
3. Had an edge in the game
4. Young woman
5. Northwestern University frat letters
6. Former Cubs pitcher, Terry ___
7. Former Cubs infielder, ___ La Russa
8. More than plump
9. Plants grass in the outfield again
10. Chicago Opera highlight
11. Chicago Bear foe
12. Award won by featured player in 1998 (Abbr.)
13. Yankees' cable TV network
21. Not straight
22. Peddle team merchandise
23. Stadium CPR pro
24. Most literal
25. No less than (2 wds.)
28. Hereditary

29. Got vengeance for a loss
30. Chicago sports announcer Grobstein
32. Fill the fans with joy
34. Clubhouse foodie
39. Cultural Revolution leader
40. *Chicago Tribune* food blog: The ___
41. Tilt
42. Players' knee surgery sites, for short
44. Cubs media guide drawing
45. Digital tomes

48. Harden
49. Player's apology (2 wds.)
51. Roman robe
52. Illinois' is the White Oak
53. Grander than grand game
54. Stat featured player led the NL in during 1998 and 2001 seasons
55. UN workers' grp.
56. Joliet prisoner
59. Bachelor's last words (2 wds.)
60. Neither's partner
61. ___ Grove Village

Outfielders' Trivia
Answers on page 148.

1. Which Cubs outfielder played 1,117 consecutive games from 1963-70?

2. Who was the Cubs outfielder, known as "Peanuts," who appeared as a youngster in Our Gang movies?

3. Sammy Sosa hit three home runs in a game three times in 2001. Who is the only other player in Major League history to do that?

4. Sammy Sosa had 146 runs and 160 RBI in 2001. Before that, who was the last player in the Big Leagues with 300+ combined runs and RBI? Hint: It was in 1949.

5. Which Cubs outfielder was the first Major League player with at least 20 home runs, 20 triples and 20 doubles in a season?

6. Which future U.S. President did former Cubs outfielder Ethan Allen mentor as Yale University's baseball coach?

7. Which Cubs outfielder in the 1980s was known as "The Sarge?"

8. Who was the left fielder the Cubs obtained in a 1953 trade, who had led the National League in home runs from 1946-52?

9. Which outfielder hit a Cubs record four pinch-hit home runs in 1999?

10. Who did the Cubs trade to the Chicago White Sox in 1992 to acquire Sammy Sosa (and Ken Patterson)?

11. Who was the Cubs outfielder who won the National League Rookie of the Year award in 1989 by hitting .293 with 24 stolen bases?

12. Which Cubs outfielder sang the national anthem before a game in 1989, a season in which he hit .324 and finished second to his teammate in Rookie of the Year voting?

13. Which Cubs outfielder became a national hero after saving a U.S. flag from being set on fire by protestors at Dodger Stadium in 1976?

14. Which Cubs outfielder had a son who hit more than 500 home runs in the Big Leagues?

15. Who was the Cubs right fielder who hit a home run in his first Major League at bat and a triple in his second at bat, both off that year's Cy Young award winner, Warren Spahn?

16. Who was the 15th highest paid player on the 1987 Cubs team who won the National League Most Valuable Player award after hitting 49 home runs and driving in 137 runs?

17. Which Cubs outfielder, who led the team in RBI in 1975 and made the National League All-Star team in '77, was a coach on the 2009 Puerto Rico World Baseball Classic squad?

18. Who made his Major League debut as an outfielder with the Cubs in 1986 and ended his career in 2005 as one of only four players in history with 500+ home runs and 3,000+ hits?

19. Which free agent did the Cubs sign to a reported eight-year, $136 million contract in 2007, the richest deal ever for the franchise?

20. Which Cubs outfielder won a silver medal at the 1996 Olympics, a bronze medal at the 2004 Olympics and gold medals at the 2006 and 2009 World Baseball Classics?

21. Which Cubs outfielder had a foul pop taken away by fan Steve Bartman in the 2003 National League Championship Series?

22. Which two-time All-Star outfielder helped the Cubs get to three World Series in the 1930s with a .309 batting average over six seasons?

23. Which outfielder played five seasons in Chicago under Cap Anson, then became the most celebrated and influential evangelist in the U.S. during the first 20 years of the 20th century?

24. Which Cubs outfielder, after being demoted to the minor leagues, became a National League umpire, a job he held for 19 years?

25. Who played for the Cleveland Rebels in the National Basketball Association's inaugural season of 1946-47, then was the Cubs' starting right fielder in 1949?

Su-Walt-Ku

Use logic to fill in the grid below so that every row, every column and every 3 x 3 box contains the letters W-A-L-T-M-O-R-Y-N, in honor of Walt Moryn, who was an outfielder with the Cubs from 1956-60. He was selected an All-Star in 1958. Solution on page 149.

A				N				Y
		Y	M		O	L		
		N	R		W	Y		
T								A
		L	Y		M	R		
		O	A		R	W		
N				L				M

Cap Anson

Chapter 7

Managers

Mike Quade was named the interim manager of the Chicago Cubs with 37 games remaining in the 2009-10 season. The "interim" tag was removed on Oct. 19, 2010. Quade, the 57th manager in franchise history, was a minor league manager for 17 seasons and the Cubs' third base coach for four years.

The club's first manager was Albert Spalding, who compiled a record of 78-47 in 1876-77 and guided Chicago to the first championship of the newly formed National League. The manager with the longest tenure and most wins is Cap Anson, who won 1,283 games over 18 seasons (1879, 1880-97). His teams won five NL titles.

Player/manager Frank Chance (1905-12) led the Cubs to four pennants and their only two World Series wins in 1907 and '08. Chance's .645 winning percentage is tops for the Cubs.

Fred Mitchell (1917-20) won the NL title in 1918 and Joe McCarthy (1926-30) won the pennant in 1929. Charlie Grimm (1932-38, 1944-49, 1960) won 946 games and three NL championships. Player/manager Gabby Hartnett (1938-40) won the 1938 pennant.

In one of the most unique managerial situations in sports history, the Cubs utilized a College of Coaches for the 1961 and '62 seasons. The Cubs rotated four managers—Vedie Himsl, Harry Craft, El Tappe and Lou Klein—in 1961 and three—Tappe, Klein and Charlie Metro—in '62.

Since then, notable managers have included Leo Durocher (1966-72), Jim Frey (1984-86), Don Zimmer (1988-91), Jim Riggleman (1995-99), Dusty Baker (2003-06) and Lou Piniella (2007-10).

Su-Pos-Ku

When managers turn in the lineup card prior to each game, each player is assigned a defensive number. The pitcher is 1, the catcher is 2, first baseman 3, second baseman 4, third baseman 5, shortstop 6, left fielder 7, center fielder 8 and right fielder 9. Use logic to fill in the grid below so that every row, every column and every 3 x 3 box contains the defensive numbers 1 through 9. Solution on page 150.

		8	6	9	2		1	
		5					8	
	6			1		9	3	
			5			3	7	
				8				
	1	6			9			
	4	7		2			9	
	8					1		
	5		9	7	6	8		

Frey-ed

Jim Frey was manager of the Cubs from 1984-86, winning the National League Manager of the Year Award in '84 after leading the Cubs to a division title (and their first postseason appearance in 39 years). The letters F-R-E-Y can be arranged to form 24 different combinations. Here are 21 of those combinations. Which three combinations are missing? Answer on page 149.

FERY	YFRE	EFRY	FYER	RYFE	FREY	REFY
FRYE	ERYF	YRFE	RYEF	YREF	EFYR	RFEY
EYFR	FYRE	RFYE	YERF	ERFY	FEYR	YFER

Managers' Mini-Crossword

Solution on page 150.

Across

1. Made MLB debut as manager on Aug. 23, 2010
6. Fond du ___, Wis.
9. Take back, in a way
10. Pitcher's stat
11. By and large (3 wds.)
13. Golfer's goal
14. Serpentine letter
15. Whiffleball, e.g.
17. Tigers on a scoreboard
18. University of Utah athlete
19. Hit on the head
21. Baffle with off-speed pitches
24. Sculler's need
25. Cry of surrender
26. North Pole toymaker
27. Played for Braves, Dodgers, Giants and Athletics before becoming a manager

Down

1. Witty remark
2. Opposite of Robert Redford's baseball character
3. Artificial playing surface
4. Morse Code dash
5. Batter's asset
6. New car possession option
7. Great philosopher
8. Fire the manager
12. Club ___ (resort)
16. NY Yankees cable network
20. Jury member
21. Opposing player
22. Training room spot
23. Genetic initials

After solving the crossword puzzle, use the letters in the grid to answer the additional clue. Transfer the letters in numbered boxes to the corresponding blanks below. (Or answer the additional clue first to help you solve the crossword puzzle.)

Team's manager in 1960 who was the 1948 American League MVP.

___ ___ ___ ___ ___ ___ ___ ___
19 24 25 17 23 26 7   18

Piniella Wordsmith

Using the letters P-I-N-I-E-L-L-A, how many words of four or more letters can you make? We found 33 fairly common words (plus 27 not so common ones that are acceptable in a tournament game of SCRABBLE). Proper nouns, foreign words and abbreviations don't count. If you can find 25 or more words in 25 minutes, you're an All-Star Wordsmith. Solution on page 150.

Manage the Boxes

Place the names of these 19 Cubs managers into the grid, one name for each row and no more than one letter per box, so that the highlighted column reading down spells out a phrase that is related to the puzzle theme. We've given you hints on where some of the names go by putting some (but not all) of the Cs, Us, Bs and Ss in place. You must use all of the names, but not all the boxes—both to the left and right of the names—will have a letter in them. Our solution on page 151.

BAKER

BAYLOR

CHANCE

DUROCHER

ELIA

FRANKS

FREY

FRISCH

GRIMM

HACK

KENNEDY

LEFEBVRE

LOFTUS

MCCARTHY

PINIELLA

RIGGLEMAN

SPALDING

WILSON

ZIMMER

					C					
							C			
				C						
B										
	U									
						S				
					B					
						C				
		S								
							S			
				B						
				S						

Managers' Word Search

Find the Cubs managers' names in the grid on the next page. The names run up, down, sideways and diagonally. No letter is used more than once. When you have found all the names listed, there will be 43 unused letters. Starting at the top row and moving left to right, then to the second row, and so on, put the unused letters into the spaces below to reveal a hidden factoid. Solution on page 151.

AMALFITANO	FRANKS	LEFEBVRE	RIGGLEMAN
BAKER	GRIMM	LOCKMAN	SCHEFFING
BAYLOR	HARTNETT	MARSHALL	TINKER
BRESNAHAN	HORNSBY	MCCARTHY	TREBELHORN
CAVARRETTA	KENNEDY	MITCHELL	WILSON
DUROCHER	KILLEFER	PINIELLA	ZIMMER

___ ___ ___   ___ ___ ___ ___   ___ ___   ___ ___ ___

___ ___ ___ ___ ___ ___ ___ ___ ___ ___

___ ___ ___ ___ ___ ___ ___   ___ ___   ___ ___ ___ ___

___ ___ ___ ___ ___ ___ ___ ___ .

```
A  G  C  M  A  R  S  P  H  R  O  L  Y  A  B
L  R  L  A  C  K  E  O  N  R  S  D  O  N  I
L  I  S  L  N  C  R  K  E  T  U  H  E  N  W
E  M  I  A  A  N  A  K  A  R  N  K  N  R  N
I  M  R  O  S  H  N  R  O  B  I  I  A  O  N
N  F  M  B  N  I  S  C  T  G  N  L  M  H  A
I  L  Y  I  T  A  H  R  N  H  T  L  E  L  H
P  N  O  G  T  E  T  I  A  T  Y  E  L  E  A
K  O  E  C  R  C  F  I  E  M  S  F  G  B  N
E  S  T  M  K  F  H  N  F  Z  A  E  G  E  S
N  L  N  A  E  M  T  E  G  L  I  R  I  R  E
N  I  E  H  R  R  A  I  L  N  A  M  R  T  R
E  W  C  C  A  U  B  N  S  L  H  M  M  I  B
D  S  S  H  L  E  F  E  B  V  R  E  A  E  T
Y  O  R  Y  A  T  T  E  R  R  A  V  A  C  R
```

Managers' Crossword

Solution on page 152.

Across

1. 1980 World Series manager with the Royals and the Cubs manager from 1984-86
5. Needle bag
9. Downy material
14. Humdinger of a game
15. Huckleberry ___
16. Rajah's wife
17. Oil grp.
18. Try out
19. Accessory software program
20. Small lizard
22. Verb preceder
24. Bears lineman
25. Tennis match part
26. Baby's first word, maybe
29. Go around
31. Raring to go
32. Citizens Bank Park winter hrs.
33. Cubs first baseman from 1958-59 and manager from 1974-76
36. Give up the game
40. Stadium poster
41. Listen incorrectly
44. Lofty
45. Cubs manager who won division titles for three franchises
46. Flow's partner
49. Golf clubs
50. Scotch whisky name at Bernie's Tavern
52. Hungry Cubbie restaurant handout
53. When doubled, a dance
56. Game 7 of the World Series mo.
57. Oxen's harness
59. Say "@#$%!" to an umpire
61. Bay window in a Wrrigleyville townhouse
63. The game skinny
66. Teen affliction
67. Michael Moore health care flick
68. One-dish meal
69. Detroit NFL player
70. Ethyl acetate, e.g.
71. Scattered
72. Cubs pinch hitter in 1968 and manager in 1982-83

Down

1. Beats severely
2. Indian coin
3. Vote into the Baseball Hall of Fame
4. "Ugh!"
5. Young newt
6. 4-4, e.g.
7. Clear out a postgame traffic jam
8. Enthusiastic about the Cubs
9. World Series participant in 1941 and manager of the Cubs from 1977-79 and '81
10. Schoolboy
11. Below
12. Gale Sayers move
13. Ward (off)
21. Site of the College World Series
23. Finish, with "up"
27. Ice cream thickener
28. Mix
30. Scratches
31. Forgo
33. Dashboard abbr.

34. Rope-a-dope boxer
35. Sleazy newspaper
37. Electric fish
38. SS who was 0-for-22 in the '68 World Series, ___ Maxvill
39. Pitcher's stat
41. Bog down
42. Get ___ the ground floor (2 wds.)
43. Hole in the head
45. Cheese seasoner
47. Played for six AL teams before managing the Cubs from 2000-02

48. Dude
50. Day of "Pillow Talk"
51. Kick out
53. Cubs outfielder, ___ Garriott
54. Vietnam's capital
55. United Center, e.g.
56. Barely beat, with "out"
58. HR call: "___ it goodbye!"
60. Corduroy feature
62. Barely manage, with "out"
64. Small number
65. Have title to

Managers' Trivia
Answers on page 152.

1. Lou Piniella was the first player to bat for which Major League team?

2. What was the highest division finish for the Cubs in Dusty Baker's four seasons as manager?

3. Who replaced Don Zimmer as Cubs manager in May 1991?

4. Who was the manager of the Cubs' 1945 World Series team?

5. In 1961-62, the Cubs used a "College of Coaches"—11 coaches taking turns as "head coach." Who was named the full-time "head coach" for the 1963 season?

6. Who was the first African-American coach in the Major Leagues, hired by the Cubs in 1962?

7. Who was the first African-American manager in club history?

8. Who did P.K. Wrigley pull out of the broadcast booth to replace Charlie Grimm as manager in 1960?

9. Which future Cubs manager hit three home runs in his first day as a player with the Cubs in 1958?

10. Who was the Cubs first baseman who became the team's player-manager in 1951, replacing Frankie Frisch?

11. Who was the Cubs manager who resigned in the final week of the 1930 season, then took over the reins of the New York Yankees, beating the Cubs in the '32 World Series?

12. Who was the Cubs Hall of Fame shortstop who was named player-manager midway through the 1925 season?

13. Which of the Tinker-to-Evers-to-Chance trio was not the manager of the Cubs?

14. Name three of the four teams where Lou Piniella managed before joining the Cubs.

15. Who is the only Cubs manager to manage the National League All-Star team?

16. Which Major League team did former Cubs manager Jim Riggleman manage in 2010?

17. Who did the Cubs call up from their Triple-A team to replace Don Baylor as manager in 2002?

18. Which Cubs manager had appeared in the TV show *Batman* as a henchman for the Riddler?

19. Which Cubs manager was a high school teammate of Cubs General Manger Jim Frey at Weston Hills in Cincinnati?

20. Who said (with 46 bleeps deleted): "The 3,000 fans who have been watching us each day have been very negative and expecting too much. Why don't they rip me instead of the ballplayers? Eighty-five percent of the world is working, but the 15 percent who come out to Wrigley Field have nothing better to do than heap abuse and criticism on the team. Why don't they go out and look for jobs?"

21. Which former Cubs manager was manager of China's Olympic baseball team for the 2008 games in Beijing?

22. Which future Cubs manager was nicknamed "The All-American Out" by New York Yankees teammate Babe Ruth?

23. Which National League team did Leo Durocher manage the same season he was fired by the Cubs?

24. Which future Cubs manager was on base (scoring the game-tying run) when Bobby Thompson hit the "Shot Heard 'Round the World?"

25. Which Cubs manager was known as "The Stick" in his playing days with the Pittsburgh Pirates, Los Angeles Dodgers, New York Yankees and Detroit Tigers?

Su-Do-Fri

Use logic to fill in the boxes so every row, column and 2 x 3 box contains the letters F-R-I-S-C-H, in honor of Frank Frisch, the Cubs manager from 1949-51. Solution on page 150.

		R			
	H	C	F		
		H	I	S	
	S	F	C		
		I	H	C	
			R		

Ryne Sandberg

Chapter 8

By the Numbers

The Cubs have retired six uniform numbers, honoring seven superstars:

10 Ron Santo
14 Ernie Banks
23 Ryne Sandberg
26 Billy Williams
31 Ferguson Jenkins and Greg Maddux
42 Jackie Robinson (all MLB teams)

Those numbers are visible on flags at Wrigley Field flying atop the foul poles.

Other numbers in Cubs history are just as recognizable:

66 Home runs that Sammy Sosa hit in 1998.
191 RBI that Hack Wilson had in 1930, a Major League record. (For 69 years, it was presumed that he had 190 RBI that season, but research revealed that the statisticians of the day had shorted him. The official record was changed in 1999.)
20 Strike outs that Kerry Wood had in his fifth big league start in 1998, tying the MLB record (and setting the MLB rookie record).
116 Wins by the 1906 Cubs, a team record.
103 Losses by the 1962 and '66 Cubs, a team record.
1969 The year of "The Collapse." The Cubs were in first place by 8 1/2 games on Aug. 19, but fell to the "Amazin' Mets."
1945 The last time the Cubs played in the World Series.
1908 The last time the Cubs won a World Series.

Su-Tewks-Ku

Use logic to fill in the grid below so that every row, every column and every 3 x 3 box contains the letters T-E-W-K-S-B-U-R-Y, in honor of Bob Tewksbury, a Cubs pitcher in 1987-88, who later played himself in the movie "The Scout". Solution on page 153.

E		W			K			
	T			U				R
				T		W		
	E		T					K
		K				T		
Y				W		U		
	U		E					
K				S			B	
			K			S		Y

Su-Ple-Ku

Use logic to fill in the boxes so every row, column and 2 x 3 box contains the letters P-L-E-S-A-C, in honor of Dan Plesac, a Cubs pitcher in 1993-94 and later a broadcaster with Sportsnet Chicago. Solution on page 153.

C				E	
S					A
A				C	E
L	C				P
P					C
	A				L

Go Figure

1. Take the distance, in feet, from first base to
    second base...   _____

2. Subtract Ernie Banks' uniform number...   _____

3. Subtract the number of home runs Sammy Sosa
    hit in 1998...   _____

4. Multiply by the number of World Series titles
    for the Cubs...   _____

5. Subtract the record number of strike outs
    Kerry Wood had in a 1998 game...   _____

6. Divide by the number of Gold Gloves Ron Santo won
    with the Cubs...   _____

Your answer should be equal to the uniform number of Don Zimmer
when he was manager of the Cubs. Answer on page 153.

Ifs and Thens

Complete this puzzle to reveal a four-digit number. Why is that
number significant in Cubs history?

$$\overline{\quad} \quad \overline{\quad} \quad \overline{\quad} \quad \overline{\quad}$$
$$1 \qquad 2 \qquad 3 \qquad 4$$

*   If second baseman Mike Fontenot wore uniform number 17 in
    2010, then the 4th number is 8; if he wore number 24, then
    the 2nd number is 7.
*   If the Cubs' team record for most home runs in a game is
    5, then the 1st number is 2; if the record is 7, then the 2nd
    number is 9.
*   If Billy Williams' career batting average with the Cubs was
    higher than .300, then the 3rd number is 3; if it was lower than
    .300, then the 1st number is 1.
*   If Greg Maddux had more than 1,500 strike outs in his 10
    seasons with the Cubs, then the 4th number is 4; if he had
    fewer than 1,500, then the 3rd number is 0.

Solution on page 153.

Add It Up

Here are Cubs who successfully wore uniform numbers 1 through 9:

1 Kosuke Fukedome

2 Billy Herman

3 Kiki Cuyler

4 Ralph Kiner

5 Riggs Stephenson

6 Stan Hack

7 Jody Davis

8 Andre Dawson

9 Gabby Hartnett

Now enter the numbers 1 through 9 into the box so that each column, each row and both long diagonals add up to 15. And who wore uniform number 15 best for the Cubs? Maybe Pat Malone. (We've got you started by inserting the numbers 1 and 2.)
Solution on page 153.

		1
2		

By the Numbers
Mini-Crossword

Solution on page 153.

Across

1. Number of Gold Gloves won by Ernie Banks
4. Doing a farrier's job at Arlington Park
8. Wall covering hanger
9. Goes back to the base on a fly ball
10. Rams' mates
12. Work unit
13. Floral necklace
14. Guitarist Lofgren
16. Billy Goat Curse, e.g.
17. A planet
19. Bad pun
20. Most steals of home in one game, by Joe Tinker

Down

1. Cry over a dropped pop-up
2. Society page word in the *Chicago Tribune*
3. Dublin's land
4. Avoiding waste
5. Bargainer at the box office
6. Film studio that released "Sex and the City" and "Wedding Crashers"
7. Wrigley's outfield grass compared to your lawn, probably
9. Ron Santo's uniform number
11. Cubs record for most hits in a game (held by 10 players)
15. Good name for a Dalmatian
16. 2007 film starring Ellen Page
18. Shooting marble

After solving the crossword puzzle, use the letters in the grid to answer the additional clue. Transfer the letters in numbered boxes to the corresponding blanks below. (Or answer the additional clue first to help you solve the crossword puzzle.)

Cubs second baseman who became the 1997 American League Manager of the Year.

$$\overline{}\ \overline{}\ \overline{}\ \overline{}\ \overline{}\ \overline{}\ \overline{}$$
16   1   5   14   4   1   6

By the Numbers Word Search

Find the Cubs players' names in the letter grid. The names run up, down, sideways and diagonally. Some of the names overlap. Solution on page 154.

```
I K I S T E P H E N S O N L H
L U O D L W I T H O R N S B Y
W S M A I L L I W S R H B D V
A H K C A H G M B K E G N F O
L A K E L L Y S S R U U O L M
B E L G R E B D N A S A S U G
R O R S N R T L I L C V L N I
C P O O S I P O K C H M I D J
B R O W N U L G N C E D W G H
Z C T K U G O R E H L S I R E
H S E N R A B A J A A J E E P
A R K I V M N N P N X M P N P
N O M N R Q N S T C I M M N P
D E D T A Y L O R E L Y U C D
S R E V E B N N W I J K E A M
```

ANSON	EVERS	KUSH	SPALDING
BANKS	GOLDSMITH	LUNDGREN	STEPHENSON
BARNES	GORE	MAGUIRE	TAYLOR
BROWN	GRIMES	REUSCHEL	TINKER
CHANCE	HACK	ROOT	VAUGHN
CLARKSON	HANDS	SANDBERG	WEIMER
COLE	HORNSBY	SANTO	WICKER
COONEY	JENKINS	SMITH	WILLIAMS
CUYLER	KELLY	SOSA	WILSON

Rick Sutcliffe

By the Numbers Trivia

Answers on page 154.

1. 8, a Cubs record
   a. Home runs leading off games by Rick Monday
   b. Home runs in a four-game series by Andre Dawson
   c. Home runs vs. one team in a season by Hank Sauer

2. 23, a Cubs record
   a. Most consecutive games won by Rick Sutcliffe
   b. Most losses in a season by Tom Hughes
   c. Most consecutive successful stolen base attempts by Eric Young

3. 53, a Cubs record
   a. Wins by Hall of Fame pitcher John Clarkson in 1885
   b. Dave Kingman's home runs in 1979
   c. The fewest number of wins by the Cubs in 1966

4. 27 by the Cubs, tying a National League record
   a. Runners left on base in a 14-inning game
   b. Players used in a game
   c. Singles in a nine-inning game

5. 17, a Major League record
   a. Carlos Zambrano's strike outs in his first Big League start
   b. Number of innings played in a day game
   c. Consecutive games with an RBI by Ray Grimes in 1922

6. 12, tying a Major League record
   a. Consecutive games throwing a shutout by Dizzy Dean in 1938
   b. Consecutive seasons leading the Big Leagues in RBI by Hack Wilson, 1925-36
   c. Consecutive plate appearances with a hit by Johnny Kling in 1902

7. 8, a World Series record
   a. Lead (8-0) the Cubs blew in a 1929 game
   b. RBI in a 1908 game by Frank Chance
   c. Consecutive strike outs in a 1945 game by Hank Wyse

8. 6, tying a Major League record
   a. Doubles in a game by Ron Santo in 1967
   b. Consecutive team games with a save by Rod Beck in 1998
   c. Consecutive at bats with a home run by Cap Anson in 1887

9. .335, a National League high
   a. Bill Buckner's fielding percentage in 1980
   b. Derrek Lee's batting average in 2005
   c. Aramis Ramirez's slugging percentage in 2009

10. 273, a Major League record
    a. Consecutive fielding chances without an error by a pitcher
       by Claude Passeau from 1941-46
    b. Strike outs in a season by a relief pitcher by Kerry Wood in
       2003
    c. Career home runs by a pitcher by Ferguson Jenkins

11. 545, most home runs in a Cubs uniform
    a. Ernie Banks
    b. Sammy Sosa
    c. Billy Williams

12. 400, most stolen bases in a Cubs uniform
    a. Joe Tinker
    b. Johnny Evers
    c. Frank Chance

13. .403 on base percentage, highest in a Cubs uniform
    a. Hack Wilson
    b. Bill Lange
    c. Glenn Beckert

14. 1,815, most strike outs as a batter in a Cubs uniform
    a. Sammy Sosa
    b. Gabby Hartnett
    c. Don Kessinger

15. 48, most shutouts in a Cubs uniform
    a. Orval Overall
    b. Ed Reulbach
    c. Mordecai Brown

16. 271, most home runs allowed in a Cubs uniform
    a. Ferguson Jenkins
    b. Greg Maddux
    c. Steve Trachsel

17. 53, saves in a season by a Cubs player
    a. Bruce Sutter
    b. Lee Smith
    c. Randy Myers

18. 32.2, consecutive scoreless innings pitched by a Cubs reliever
    a. Tom Gordon
    b. Warren Brustar
    c. Joe Borowski

19. 729, most errors in a Cubs uniform
    a. Tom Burns
    b. Billy Herman
    c. Shawon Dunston

20. 77, most runners caught stealing by a Cubs catcher
    a. Todd Hundley
    b. Joe Girardi
    c. Michael Barrett

21. Reason for Bill Voiselle wearing uniform number 96 with the Cubs
    a. That was the speed of his fastball.
    b. He was from Ninety-Six, South Carolina.
    c. It was the number of losses the Cubs had the year before.

22. Reason for Chris Krug wearing uniform number 25 with the Cubs
    a. He was born on Christmas 1939.
    b. He was the last man named to the 25-man roster in 1965.
    c. He was standing in line behind the player who got number 24 and in front of the player who got number 26.

23. Only player to wear uniform number 94 with the Cubs
    a. Felix Heredia
    b. Daniel Garibay
    c. Robert Machado

24. The two players who have worn number 99 with the Cubs
    a. Todd Hundley
    b. So Taguchi
    c. Felix Sanchez

25. Most recent player to wear number 13 with the Cubs
    a. Ryan Freel
    b. Starlin Castro
    c. Turk Wendell

By the Numbers Crossword
Solution on page 154.

Across

1. French farewell
6. Cubs' career victory leader among pitchers
10. Junk e-mail
14. Cubs' career total bases leader
15. Numbered composition
16. Neighborhood, like Wrigleyville
17. Person with a mike
18. Bit of smoke
19. "___ of the Flies"
20. In the center of the game
21. Quitter's word
22. Untamed
23. Cambridge sch.
24. First-rate player
25. Hamburger topper
26. Afresh
28. Mire
29. Gumshoe
30. Player's stick-to-itiveness
31. Cubs 1B Pagel or P Adams
33. Undertaking
34. Concurs
37. P Warner or Aker
40. Bar mitzvah, e.g.
41. Video recorders, briefly
44. Pitcher's stat
45. Tit for ___
46. "The Taming of the ___"
47. NYSE rival
49. Homophone for (Manny) Trillo
51. Once around the track
53. Cubs outfielder known as the Hoosier Hammer, Chuck ___

54. "That's a ___!"
55. Manicurist's tool
56. "Cast Away" setting
57. Goes quickly
58. DuPage County city that is home to Benedictine University
59. Spick-and-span
60. Part of 23-Across: Abbr.
61. Cubs career leader in hits and RBI
62. Wood cutters
63. Cubs career home run leader
64. Chew like a beaver

Down

1. Crosswise, on deck
2. Obstructing, like a beaver
3. Dugout provoker
4. Barely managed, with "out"
5. "What's the ___?"
6. Martin's "Laugh-In" partner
7. Offer one's two cents
8. Dethrone the pennant winner
9. Cooking meas.
10. Illinois birthplace of William Jennings Bryan
11. Proportionately (2 wds.)
12. Freshens the outfield, in a way
13. Cubs third baseman from 1974-76 who won a World Series with the Pirates
21. Playing hard to get
22. Driving hazard
24. Choir voice
25. Snitched on a teammate
27. Candle cord

28. French cheese
31. Make a sweater
32. Perform at the Goodman Theatre
33. Bygone despot
35. Mideast hot spot
36. Say again
37. Cubs career strike out leader
38. Body of water near the Caspian (2 wds.)
39. Court precedent (2 wds.)
42. ESPN Chicago reporter, ____ Isaacson

43. Drink the Gatorade
45. Bleacher Bum bronzed look
46. Bit of a beer
48. Atkins and Jenny Craig, e.g.
49. Player's lock of hair
50. Bob Marley fan
52. Hammer parts
54. Port authority?
55. Certain Scandinavian
57. Towel stitching
58. Fall behind in the standings

Wrigley Field

Chapter 9

Wrigley Field

Weeghman Park was built in six weeks in 1914 at a cost of about $250,000 by Charles Weeghman, who owned the Chicago Whales of the Federal League. Following the 1915 season, the Federal League folded. Weeghman immediately joined forces with William Wrigley Jr. and bought the Chicago Cubs. They moved the Cubs from the West Side Grounds into Weeghman Park in 1916. From 1920-26, the stadium was called Cubs Park. It became Wrigley Field following the 1926 season.

"The Friendly Confines" is bound by Clark Street (west), Addison Street (south), Waveland Avenue (north) and Sheffield Avenue (east) in the Lakeview area of the north side of Chicago.

Wrigley Field is the second oldest ballpark in the Major Leagues and is easily identified by its ivy covered brick walls, iconic red marquee, hand turned scoreboard, unpredictable wind off nearby Lake Michigan, festive bleachers fans, a white W flag following Cubs wins (and a blue L flag following losses) and rooftop seating on the buildings across the street. Wrigley Field did not install permanent lights until 1988.

The current capacity of 41,460 makes Wrigley Field the 10th smallest park in the Major Leagues. The dimensions are: 355 feet to left, 400 feet to center and 353 feet to right.

Wrigley Field also has been the home of the Chicago Bears (NFL) and Chicago Sting (NASL). In recent years, the stadium has played host to concerts, a Chicago Blackhawks (NHL) game and a Northwestern-Illinois college football game.

Wrigley Categories

For each of the categories listed, come up with a word or phrase beginning with each letter on the left. Our solution on page 155.

	Baseball Term	Cubs Pitcher
W		
R		
I		
G		
L		
E		
Y		

	Cubs Outfielder	Chicago Street
W		
R		
I		
G		
L		
E		
Y		

One and Only

Hidden in the grid is one and only one complete WRIGLEY. See if you can find it. Solution on page 155.

```
W  R  I  G  W  R  E  L  G  I  R  W  Y  W  L
R  R  I  G  L  E  Y  W  R  I  G  L  Y  R  W
I  W  I  Y  W  R  I  R  L  E  L  I  L  R  R
L  G  I  G  R  R  W  I  W  G  W  R  I  G  Y
G  W  L  E  L  W  I  G  I  Y  R  G  W  L  E
E  R  R  W  G  E  L  R  L  Y  G  L  Y  E  L
Y  E  L  L  I  R  W  L  E  L  R  R  Y  Y  I
W  R  G  R  L  W  R  E  E  E  Y  E  R  W  R
Y  R  L  I  L  L  I  Y  W  L  L  R  W  R  W
E  W  I  W  R  I  G  R  R  G  Y  I  E  I  E
L  E  Y  G  E  W  L  L  I  G  R  G  L  G  L
G  W  R  Y  W  Y  E  R  G  I  W  R  G  I  G
W  R  I  G  L  E  W  R  E  R  I  R  I  E  I
R  R  G  W  I  L  L  E  L  W  G  L  R  Y  R
W  R  I  G  I  E  Y  W  Y  R  I  G  W  R  W
```

Wrigley Field Crossword

Solution on page 155.

Across

1. Verbally joust with an umpire
5. Assist in a clubhouse wrongdoing
9. Fielder's mitt
14. Between innings ditty
15. Broadway musical blamed for the Red Sox selling Babe Ruth to the Yankees: ___ Nanette (2 wds.)
16. Lassoed
17. Team photographer's camera part
18. Former Cubs catcher, ___ Hundley
19. Sharp
20. Unbeatable team, to the Cubs
22. Street on the southside of Wrigley Field
24. Say hi at the turnstiles
25. University of Chicago home: ___ Park
26. Kentucky horse race
29. Three-bagger
34. Spoiled, like old beer
37. Must-haves, like a new Cubs jersey
39. Shake up
40. Wrigley Field feature (3 wds.)
44. Retain a Cubs home run ball
45. Not as common, like a perfect game
46. Batter's asset
47. Typos in the game program
50. More modern, like U.S. Cellular Field
52. Once, long ago
54. Soriano, Ditka or Jordan, e.g.
58. Family with the longest continuous operation of a franchise in one city (1921-81)
62. Annoying, like a rain delay
64. Celebrate a division championship
65. Infielder Mark De ___

67. On the briny
68. Like "The Bearman"
69. Randy Johnson: The Big ___
70. Lascivious look from the pitcher
71. Office copier need
72. Sit for a team photo
73. Drops the ball

Down

1. NASL team that played at Wrigley
2. More refined, like bottled water
3. Japanese baseball cartoon art
4. Tend to a bald spot in the outfield grass
5. Opposed to night games
6. Sounds of displeasure from the bleachers
7. Finish the season
8. Chicago daily newspaper from 1970-74
9. Newspaper critic, often
10. Centers of activity, like pitcher's mounds
11. Numbered composition for the CSO
12. Emphatic no from the GM
13. First place?
21. Front office shorthand taker
23. Banned pesticide for the ground crew
25. Outfield irrigation tap
27. Team minister, briefly
28. "Cold one"
30. PNC Bank offering, for short
31. It's topped with flags of retired numbers: Foul ___
32. Easter flower
33. "Cubs win! What ___ is new?"
34. Two-wheel transport to the game
35. State confidently, like "Wait 'til next year!"

36. Former Cubs coach, Duffy ___
38. Sun-cracked, like Chicago in July
41. Team bean counter, for short
42. Morning moisture on the outfield grass
43. Cubs to doubters: The Big Blue Train ___
48. The T of ATM, a Wrigley Field amenity
49. Stadium map designation: "You ___ here"
51. Selling the Cubs again
53. Original Pancake House topper
55. Not a winner

56. Mideast VIP (Var.)
57. NFL team that played at Wrigley
58. Order in the court?
59. Iowa Cubs foe in the Pacific Coast League
60. Former Cubs shortstop, ___ De Jesus
61. Former Cubs manager, ___ Michael
62. Michigan Avenue clothing store: ___ on Melrose
63. Evaluate a prospective player
66. A Beatle bride

Word Cub-e

Starting anywhere in the box, use adjacent letters—vertically, horizontally or diagonally—to make as many words as you can from the letters in FRIENDLY CONFINES. Words need to be three or more letters and cannot use the same letter cube more than once per word. No proper nouns, hyphenated or foreign words and no slang. We found about 55 "common" words, but there are a total of 102 words that are in "The Official SCRABBLE Players Dictionary." Find 40 words in 30 minutes to earn induction into the Solving Hall of Fame. List of words on page 156.

F	R	I	E
N	D	L	Y
C	O	N	F
I	N	E	S

Wrigley Field Mini-Crossword

Solution on page 156.

Across

1. Had pizza in the bleachers
4. Tennis match part
7. Hair straightening item
9. Bygone royal
10. Test choice
11. Facilitate
12. Democrats' political symbol
14. Avenue beyond the rightfield wall
17. Hamburger topper at the ballpark
18. Trails off
19. Colonel or captain
23. Aid in crime
24. ___ gin fizz at Cubby Bear Bar
25. It was dropped in the '60s
26. Unit of work

Down

1. Pretend to get hit by a pitch
2. Blue Jays on the scoreboard
3. Relative of an ostrich at Lincoln Park Zoo
4. Concession stand frozen drink order
5. Artist's stand
6. ABBA lyric: "But then, ___ never shared our love..."
8. Confined to a mattress
9. Ticket discount recipients, usually
13. Frequently, in verse
14. Swipe second base
15. Redford in "The Natural"
16. Attach to, like a reporter
20. A pint, maybe, at Wrigley Field Bar & Grill
21. Neither's partner
22. It's tapped at the concession stands

After solving the crossword puzzle, use the letters in the grid to answer the additional clue. Transfer the letters in numbered boxes to the corresponding blanks below. (Or answer the additional clue first to help you solve the crossword puzzle.)

Cubs second baseman at Wrigley Field from 1965-73, he was a four-time All-Star.

___ ___ ___ ___ ___ ___ ___
 8   5   7   22   3   19   17

Wrigley Field Trivia
Answers on page 157.

1. Who was the future Cubs player (then with the New York Mets in 1976) who hit what is believed to be the longest home run in Wrigley Field history—550 feet over Waveland Avenue?

2. How many home runs were hit to tie the National League record for home runs in a game in the Cubs' 23-22, 10-inning loss to the Philadelphia Phillies at Wrigley Field on May 17, 1979?

3. Who was the Billy Goat Tavern owner who was asked to leave Wrigley Field during the 1945 World Series because he had a smelly goat with him? Bonus points if you know the name of his goat, too.

4. Who was the 91-year-old fan who flipped the ceremonial light switch for the first Cubs game under lights at Wrigley Field?

5. When was the first night baseball game at Wrigley Field?

6. In 1941, the Cubs were the first Big League team to install what at Wrigley Field?

7. True or False? Wrigley Field was the first stadium with bat racks in the dugout.

8. True or Fasle? *The Home Run Derby* TV show (still shown on ESPN Classic) was filmed at Wrigley Field in 1959.

9. When did Babe Ruth hit his "called shot" home run in a World Series game at Wrigley Field?

10. Who tied the Major League record for most hits in a career with No. 4,191 at Wrigley Field on Sept. 8, 1985?

11. Who was the Wrigley Field ball girl who was fired in 1986 for posing nude in *Playboy*?

12. Has Astroturf ever been installed at Wrigley Field?

13. Who was the Cubs' Wrigley Field PA announcer from 1916-74 who started each game with the announcement, "Attention! Attention, please! Have your pencils and scorecards ready, and I will give you the correct lineups for today's game."

14. Who was the Wrigley Field clubhouse attendant/equipment manager from 1943-2008 who was known for wearing a white fishing cap?

15. Which athletic apparel company had its company name and logo on the outfield doors at Wrigley Field in 2010?

16. What is the meaning of "EAMUS CATULI!" and "AC0164101" seen on signs on the roof of the building at 3633 Sheffield Avenue and visible inside Wrigley Field?

17. Who was one of the creators of the long-running stage play "Bleacher Bums" (based on life in the Wrigley Field bleachers) who went on to star in the TV series *Joan of Arcadia* and *Criminal Minds*?

18. When was the last time Wrigley Field was the site of the Major League All-Star Game?

19. What is the color of the flag and the letter W that is raised at Wrigley Field after a Cubs win?

20. Which Chicago Bears star rushed for a record-tying six touchdowns at Wrigley Field in the Bears 61-20 victory over the San Francisco 49ers?

21. Which musician was the first to use Wrigley Field as a concert venue in 2005?

22. Which Cubs great was honored with a statue outside Wrigley Field that was unveiled on Mar. 31, 2008?

23. Which former Cubs player was the manager of the Class A Peoria Chiefs when they played the Kane County Cougars in the first minor league baseball game at Wrigley Field in 2008?

24. Which two Big Ten football teams played a game at Wrigley Field in 2010?

25. Which Chicago Transit Authority train line has a stop at Addison, one block east of Wrigley Field?

Su-Wain-Ku

Use logic to fill in the grid below so that every row, every column and every 3 x 3 box contains the letters W-A-I-N-H-O-U-S-E, in honor of Dave Wainhouse, a free agent pitcher signed by the Cubs for the 2001 season. Solution on page 156.

E		I		N				O
	O				U	E		
	W		I			S		
	U				S			I
A				O				E
S			W				O	
		O			N		E	
		H	E				A	
U				A		I		W

Bruce Sutter

Chapter 10

Extra Innings

Think of the Chicago Cubs and most fans conjure up images of "Loveable Losers," pinstripe uniforms and Wrigley Field. Others identify the team by the TV announcers.

Thanks to Chicago superstation WGN and its sister radio station, the Cubs have been beamed into homes throughout the country. And Harry Caray, Jack Brickhouse, Lou Boudreau, Vince Lloyd, Steve Stone and Ron Santo have been as much a part of the team as Ernie Banks, Bruce Sutter and Geovany Soto.

It was Caray who made the singing of "Take Me Out To The Ball Game" a Wrigley Field fixture during the seventh inning stretch.

Cubs fans sitting in the bleachers have become famous worldwide. The "Bleacher Bums" are known for heckling and dumping beer on opposing outfielders, throwing visiting team home run balls back onto the field and working on their tans at day games. The group even inspired a Broadway play, "The Bleacher Bums."

Why have the Cubs not been to the World Series since 1945? Many will say it's the "Curse of the Billy Goat." That was when the Cubs management asked Billy Goat Tavern owner Billy Sianis to remove his pet goat from Wrigley Field due to the animal's odor bothering other fans. According to legend, an irate Sianis said, "Them Cubs, they aren't gonna win no more." The Curse was born.

The Cubs haven't been to a World Series since 1945, but that hasn't prevented the Cubs from winning the championship in three films: *Rookie of the Year, Back to the Future Part II* and *Taking Care of Business*.

Missing Cubs

Place the letters C-U-B-S, once each, in any order, to form a fairly common eight-letter word in each line. Solution on page 157.

1. ___ ___ ___ K E T ___
2. ___ E ___ A ___ ___ E
3. A ___ D ___ ___ T ___
4. ___ A ___ K ___ P ___
5. ___ I ___ ___ ___ I T
6. ___ O ___ N ___ E ___
7. ___ ___ N ___ H E ___
8. ___ O M ___ ___ ___ T
9. O ___ ___ ___ ___ R E
10. ___ ___ ___ J E ___ T

Su-Val-Ku

Use logic to fill in the boxes so every row, column and 2 x 3 box contains the letters V-A-L-D-E-S, in honor of Pedro Valdes, a Cubs outfielder in 1996 and '98. Besides playing in the Major Leagues, Valdes also played professionally in Japan, Korea and Mexico. Solution on page 158.

		A	V		
V	L		D		S
			E	V	
	E	V			
E		S		D	A
		D	S		

Bare Bones Crossword 1

Solution on page 158.

Across

1. Wrigley Field team
5. Carlos Marmol's October birthstone
6. Former Cubs pitcher Jim Kremmel, as a collegian at UNM
7. Yogi Berra: "...like deja vu all over again."

Down

1. Stadium soft drink
2. Knowledgeable about the Cubs (2 wds.)
3. "The Sultan of Swat"
4. Like an off-speed pitch

1	2	3	4
5			
6			
7			

Bare Bones Crossword 2

Solution on page 158.

Across

1. Biblical twin
5. Baby bears
6. Assist in the dugout
7. Lyric baseball poems

Down

1. Sound rebound in the empty tunnels of Wrigley Field
2. Took the team to court
3. Proficient in the field
4. Govt. alternative to FedEx

1	2	3	4
5			
6			
7			

Bare Bones Crossword 3

Solution on page 158.

Across

1. Mend the players' socks
5. CSO woodwind
6. Young boy scouts
7. Leave in, to the game program editor

Down

1. Team physicians, briefly
2. Border on Wrigley Field
3. Clubhouse cover-up
4. Home in the Illinois state tree

1	2	3	4
5			
6			
7			

Bare Bones Crossword 4

Solutionson page 158.

Across

1. Like some batters?
5. 100%
6. Tehran's land
7. Rookie reporters

Down

1. Colossal story about the team
2. Team know-it-all
3. Snag
4. Pay for playing in Japan

1	2	3	4
5			
6			
7			

Word Transformations

Change one letter at a time to transform these baseball terms into new baseball terms. Change one letter of the first word to make a new word, then another letter in the new word to make another word and so forth until you reach the new baseball term. For example, to transform FAIR to FOUL, you can change the R in FAIR to an L, making it FAIL, then change the A in FAIL to an O to make it FOIL, then change the I in FOIL to a U to make it FOUL. Each step must be a common four-letter word. No foreign words, proper nouns, abbreviations or slang are allowed. See if you can make each of these transformations in four moves. And for bonus points, see if you can make one of the words in the middle of the transformation a baseball term, too. Our solutions are on page 158.

WALK	HITS	BELT
_____	_____	_____
_____	_____	_____
_____	_____	_____
BUNT	GAME	RUNS

BASE	SLID	CUBS
_____	_____	_____
_____	_____	_____
_____	_____	_____
OUTS	TEAM	HOPE

Extra Innings Mini-Crossword

Solution on page 158.

Across

1. With 28-Across, long-time voice of the Cubs
6. J. Edgar Hoover's org.
9. Boredom in the bleachers
10. Stately tree
11. Postage indicator
12. Leo Durocher's nickname, with "The"
13. Sacred hymn
15. P David Pavlas' Rice University mascot
17. Cook in the microwave
18. Certain sorority member
20. School org.
21. Standoffish
25. Moray, e.g.
26. Exit the ballpark
27. Rally song: "We ___ Family"
28. See 1-Across

Down

1. "For ___ a jolly..."
2. Hill dweller
3. Genetic initials
4. Muss up a uniform
5. Putter's woes
6. Mac
7. FOX Sports' airborne camera location
8. Little troublemaker
14. Flowering shrub
15. Aquatic mammal
16. Humpback, e.g.
19. Locker room powder
20. Podded plant
22. Stick in the water
23. Egg cells
24. "30 Rock" creator, Tina ___

After solving the crossword puzzle, use the letters in the grid to answer the additional clue. Transfer the letters in numbered boxes to the corresponding blanks below. (Or answer the additional clue first to help you solve the crossword puzzle.)

Cubs starting shortstop between Garciaparra and Cedano.

___ ___ ___ ___ ___
20   9   3   25 17

Extra Innings Trivia
Answers on page 160.

1. After Harry Caray's death, who was the first guest singer of "Take Me Out To The Ball Game" on Opening Day 1998?

2. Who were the three future Pro Football Hall of Fame members who played in the Cubs-Cincinnati Reds game on July 2, 1917?

3. Who was Major League Baseball's first Singapore-born player? Hint: He was a rookie outfielder with the Cubs in 1996.

4. Which Cubs pitcher gave up a home run in a 1995 game, then was attacked on the mound by a fan?

5. Who played right field for the Chicago White Sox in an exhibition game with the Cubs at Wrigley Field on Apr. 7, 1994?

6. In 1971, who were the brothers that played for the Cubs, the first set of brothers to play together for the Cubs since 1894?

7. Where was Harry Caray working when the Cubs hired him in November 1981?

8. Which sport did Cubs President Jim Finks play professionally before joining the Cubs?

9. Who was the Cubs player who was traded for himself in 1987?

10. Which Cubs player was the first to wear an earflap on his batting helmet?

11. What is the name of the Cubs spring training stadium in Mesa, Ariz.?

12. What was added to the Cubs' home uniforms for the first time in 1957?

13. True or False? In 1940, the Cubs were the first Major League team to wear sleeveless jerseys.

14. True or False? In 1939, the Cubs and Brooklyn Dodgers played a doubleheader using bright yellow baseballs.

15. Which Chicago radio station (still in existence) was the first to broadcast a Cubs game in 1924?

16. Did the Cubs ever have a live bear cub as a mascot?

17. Who penned the line: "Tinker to Evers to Chance?"

18. What stands now at Polk and Wolcott Streets where the Cubs' West Side Grounds was from 1893-1915?

19. Match each city/state with the team's nickname and minor league level for the Cubs minor league affiliates in 2010:

Boise	Chiefs	AAA
Daytona	Cubs	AA
Dominican	Cubs	A
Iowa	Cubs	A
Mesa	Cubs	A
Peoria	Hawks	Rookie
Tennessee	Smokies	Rookie

20. Who was the Cubs relief pitcher in 1972 who had been a punter on Notre Dame's football team?

21. Who was the Cubs relief pitcher from 2008-10 who had been a wide receiver on Notre Dame's football team?

22. Which Cubs announcer popularized the phrase "Hey, hey!"

23. Where did the Cubs open their 2000 regular season?

24. The 1981 World Series included seven former Cubs on the rosters of the New York Yankees and Los Angeles Dodgers. Name four of those players.

25. Who did the Cubs select in the first round of the 2010 Major League Baseball draft?

Destined to be a Cub

There are several Cubs players who have the letters C, U, B and S in their name. See if you can identify these players by filling in the rest of the letters in their names. Warning: Not all of the Cs, Us, Bs and Ss in a name are given. Answers on page 158.

1. Hall of Fame outfielder who played with the Cubs in 1960-61.

   __ __ C __ __ __   __ S __ B U __ __

2. Pitched for the Cubs from 1991-93, he was an NL All-Star with the Phillies in '95.

   __ __ __ __ __ C __ __ __ __

   S __ __ __ U __ B

3. Knuckleball reliever with the Cubs from 1961-63, he pitched four games in the '64 World Series with St. Louis.

   B __ __ __ __ __   S C __ U __ __ __

4. Cubs third baseman from 1992-95; in college at Stanford, he was the roommate of QB great John Elway.

   S __ __ __ __   B U __ C __ __ __ __

5. Outfielder with the Cubs in 1995-96, he tied for the team season high with seven triples in '95.

   S C __ __ __   B U __ __ __ __ __

6. Had 300 saves in his career (1976-88), he pitched for the Cubs from 1976-80.

   B __ __ C __   S U __ __ __ __

7. Cubs shortstop from 1943-45; he also played for the Pirates and Boston Bees in his career.

   B __ __ __   S C __ U __ __ __ __

8. Cubs catcher from 1951-54, he played in two World Series with the Brooklyn Dodgers.

   B __ U C __ 　 __ __ __ __ __ __ S

9. Hit .306 as a Cubs rookie outfielder in 1934; in '38 he was traded to the Cardinals for Dizzy Dean.

   __ U __ __ 　 S __ __ __ __ B __ C __

10. Hit .167 as a Cubs rookie outfielder in 2006; in '07 he was traded to the Reds for Marcos Mateo.

    B U __ __ 　 C __ __ __ S

Su-Do-Bol

Use logic to fill in the grid below so that every row, every column and every 3 x 3 box contains the letters J-I-M-B-O-L-G-E-R, in honor of Jim Bolger, an outfielder with the Cubs from 1955-58. Solution on page 159.

O					L		I	
	R			G				M
		G	I					
		I	R					G
	G						R	
M						O	E	
					B	J		
J				L			M	
	B		E					L

Extra Innings Crossword

Solution on page 159.

Across

1. Cubs manager in 2010-11
6. Clump of mashed potatoes
10. With 64-Across, what Wrigley Field was called from 1920-26
14. City-like
15. Illinois State Fair attraction
16. ___ retentive
17. Player's representative
18. Angers
19. Agitate
20. "Are we there ___?"
21. Perlman of "Cheers"
23. Holed out from on the green
25. Not hearing
26. Just manage, with "out"
27. Cubs outfielder who saved an American flag
30. Spanish rice dishes
34. German sub
35. Comics shriek
36. Doctrine: Suffix
37. Bloody
38. Cubs TV home
39. "Do ___ others..."
40. Catch
41. "Andy Capp" cartoonist, ___ Smythe
42. Japanese League left-handed P signed by the Cubs in 1999, Doug ___
43. Like a slingshot
46. Cubs General Manager in 2010
47. ___-tac-toe
48. Team photographer's camera part

49. Easy on the eyes
52. Sacrifice attempt, usually
53. Have bills
56. Dalai ___
57. Fashionable
59. "Bolero" composer
61. Ear-related
62. Dugout's tall tale teller
63. Render defenseless
64. See 10-Across
65. Latin 101 verb
66. Cubs 2B in 2009 who became the first batter in the new Yankee Stadium

Down

1. Wharf
2. Encourage
3. Assist in a locker room wrongdoing
4. P Serafini or 2B Rohn
5. Beseech
6. Charlie Brown saying from the pitcher's mound: "Good ___!"
7. Old Italian bread?
8. Lyrical baseball lines
9. Request
10. Syndicate
11. Randy "Big ___" Johnson
12. Cotton bundle
13. Musher's transport
22. Cow chow
24. Island strings
25. June 6, 1944
27. Sticky weather in July in Chicago
28. Double-reed instruments
29. Cubs OF in 1971-72 who led the AL in stolen bases twice

30. Relief pitchers' area, briefly
31. Hit the ball hard
32. Daisylike bloom
33. Cubs' Forrest Burgess to friends
35. Omelet ingredient
38. Game day: Abbr.
39. Coffee holders
41. Reprocess your soda bottles
42. Multivitamin maker
44. Criticize a player in the media
45. Barbecue site
46. Egg layer

48. Riches
49. Alka-Seltzer sound
50. Pro ___
51. Arab ruler
52. Partiality
53. Arlington Park track shape
54. Used to be
55. Stately trees in Wrigleyville
58. Towel stitching
60. "Wheel of Fortune" purchase
    (2 wds.)

Hack Wilson

Answers

CHAPTER 1

Cubby Holes (from page 8)
WHITE STOCKINGS

Strike Three (from page 9)
iceBERG, iSOTOpe and sLEEpy all contain the name of a player on the Cubs' 2010 team. rELIAnt, sHACKles and sTINKER all contain the name of a former Cubs manager.

Su-Mac-Ku (from page 9)

History Crossword (from page 12)

Cubs Conundrum (from page 11)

2010 Team: DEMPSTER, FONTENOT, FUKUDOME, GORZELANNY, RAMIREZ, SORIANO; Hall of Famers: BANKS, HARTNETT, JENKINS, SANDBERG, WILLIAMS; Managers: DUROCHER, LOCKMAN, RIGGLEMAN, SCHEFFING; Colors: BLUE, RED, WHITE; Announcers: BRICKHOUSE, CARAY; Owner: RICKETTS. Hidden Word: NORTHSIDERS.

History Trivia (from page 15)

1. Ryne Sandberg, Rick Sutcliffe and Scott Sanderson.
2. Atlanta Braves, 3 games to 2.
3. Andy MacPhail.
4. New York Yankees.
5. 21, which ties for the longest victory streak in Major League history.
6. Joe DiMaggio, who signed with the New York Yankees in 1936.
7. The payout to the players had been significantly reduced from the previous season. The players gave in and finished the Series.
8. Babe Ruth.
9. True. On June 23, 1895, Chicago's players were arrested for "aiding and abetting the forming of a noisy crowd on a Sunday." The team's owner posted bond on site, and the game was resumed. The players were eventually exonerated, opening the door to traditional Sunday afternoon baseball games.
10. Australia, Ceylon, England, Egypt, India, Italy, France and New Zealand.
11. Three Finger Brown, Smoky Burgess, Dizzy Dean, Pickles Dillhoefer, Bull Durham, Goose Gossage, Gabby Hartnett, Peanuts Lowrey, Rabbit Maranville and Hippo Vaughn.
12. The Chicago White Sox beat the Chicago Cubs, 4 games to 2.

13. Eight-and-a-half games.
14. Lee Smith.
15. Leon Durham.
16. Sammy Sosa.
17. Soap and baking powder. In 1892, the company began packaging gum with each can of baking powder and the gum soon was more popular than the baking powder.
18. WGN-TV.
19. Founded Ameritrade, which had its roots as a small investment banking firm.
20. Steve Macko.
21. French Lick, Ind., home to basketball Hall of Famer Larry Bird.
22. Hank Borowy, who had thrown a shutout in Game 1.
23. Stan Hack 1932-47, Hack Miller 1922-25, Hack Wilson 1926-31.
24. Grover Cleveland.
25. Grover Cleveland Alexander.

**Su-Hen-Dree-Ku
(from page 18)**

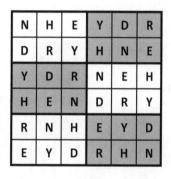

**History Mini-Crossword
(from page 19)**

Additional Clue: BASEBALL

CHAPTER 2

What's in a Name? (from page 22)

1. ANDRE DAWSON; 2. DON KESSINGER; 3. ERNIE BANKS; 4. DAVE KINGMAN; 5. JODY DAVIS; 6. RYAN DEMPSTER; 7. MARK PRIOR; 8. SAMMY SOSA; 9. BILL MADLOCK; 10. RYNE SANDBERG; 11. HOME RUN LAD; 12. BUTT RESCUER.

Apt Description (from page 25)

ERNIE BANKS

Su-Do-Curt (from page 23)

I	C	D	S	V	U	R	T	A
S	V	T	R	I	A	D	U	C
A	R	U	C	T	D	V	S	I
U	A	C	V	R	T	S	I	D
D	S	R	A	U	I	C	V	T
V	T	I	D	C	S	A	R	U
T	D	A	I	S	R	U	C	V
R	U	V	T	A	C	I	D	S
C	I	S	U	D	V	T	A	R

Su-Do-Kiki
(from page 23)

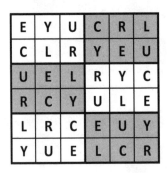

All-Stars' Mini-Crossword
(from page 24)

Additional Clue: PASSEAU

All-Stars' Trivia (from page 25)

1. The Cubs purchased Banks' contract from the Kansas City Monarchs of the Negro Leagues for $35,000.
2. Billy Herman, whose granddaughter is married to the Governor of Indiana.
3. Hoyt Wilhelm, a Hall of Famer who pitched only three of those games with the Cubs, but 361 with the White Sox.
4. Bill Madlock, who led the NL in hitting in 1975 and '76, and two more times with the Pittsburgh Pirates.

5. Clark Griffith.
6. Grace-SDSU, Holtzman-Illinois, Kingman-USC, Monday-Arizona St., Reuschel-Western Illinois.
7. Diabetes.
8. Gabby Hartnett.
9. Ivan DeJesus.
10. George Altman on Aug. 4, 1961.
11. Freddie Lindstrom, in 1924, with the New York Giants. He was 18.
12. Tony Lazzeri.
13. George Kelly, who played just one season with the Cubs (1930) and had a career batting average of .297 with 148 home runs.
14. Andre Dawson.
15. Kiki Cuyler.
16. Richie Ashburn.
17. Roger Bresnahan.
18. Don Kessinger.
19. Ferguson Jenkins.
20. Burleigh Grimes, who began his career in 1916 and played for the Cubs in 1932-33. In 1920, the spitball was banned, but 17 established pitchers were allowed to continue to throw the pitch for the remainder of their careers.
21. Jenkins-Chicago Cubs, Maddux-Los Angeles Dodgers, Santo-Chicago White Sox, Sosa-Texas Rangers, Williams-Oakland Athletics.
22. Having a professional boxing match against each other. Wilson was often getting into fisticuffs on and off the field, and Shires had been tried for manslaughter (but was acquitted) when a heckling fan died after being hit in the head with a baseball allegedly thrown by Shires.
23. Bill Nicholson, who led the NL in HR and RBI that season. After hitting four consecutive home runs in a doubleheader, he came to bat with the bases loaded and was intentionally walked.
24. Hank Sauer, who was one of the Cubs' few bright spots in the early 1950s. He was the NL MVP in 1952 when he led the League in HR (37) and RBI (121).
25. Bruce Sutter was third at 53 percent, Andre Dawson was fifth at 50 percent and Ryne Sandberg was sixth at 49 percent. Immediately behind Lee was another former Cubs player, Goose Gossage (42 percent).

Pick-Off Play (from page 29)

1. BUCKNER; 2. MADDUX; 3. HERMAN; 4. PALMEIRO; 5. WOOD; 6. SWISHER; 7. BECKERT; 8. DUNSTON; 9. HICKMAN; 10. GRACE.

All-Stars' Crossword (from page 30)

CHAPTER 3

Square Pitchers (from page 34)

1. TRACHSEL; 2. CASTILLO; 3. REUSCHEL; 4. HOLTZMAN; 5. BOROWSKI; 6. BURDETTE.

Alphabet Soup (from page 35)

1. QUEVEDO; 2. ZAMBRANO; 3. JENKINS; 4. WILCOX; 5. FARNSWORTH; 6. YOUNG; 7. DEMPSTER.

Su-Moe-Ku (from page 34)

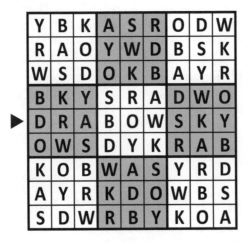

Build the Name (from page 36)

1. SUTCLIFFE; 2. MADDUX; 3. SUTTER; 4. JENKINS; 5. GORDON; 6. TIDROW; 7. REUSCHEL; 8. ELLSWORTH.

Keeping Up With the Joneses (from page 36)

1. JONES; 2. JOHNSON; 3. WILLIAMS; 4. SMITH (with two Bobs); 5. MILLER.

Pitchers' Word Search (from page 37)

Su-Bon-Ku
(from page 35)

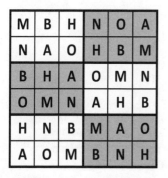

Pitchers' Mini-Crossword
(from page 38)

Additional Clue: FRENCH

S	H	E		C	A	R	D
N	A	Y		O	L	I	O
S	A	L	E	S	R	O	O	M
O	F	F		E	G	O	
S	U	T	C	L	I	F	F	E
	R	O	E		N	A	N
S	Q	U	A	S	H	E	R	S
O	U	T	S		O	S	S
B	A	H	T		P	S	I

Pitchers' Trivia (from page 39)

1. Rick Sutcliffe.
2. Jeff Pico, who was 13-12 with the Cubs in three Big League seasons.
3. Carlos Silva.
4. Sam Jones, who always pitched with a toothpick in his mouth, threw his gem May 12, 1955.
5. Lon Warneke, who played in the first All-Star Game in 1933 and umpired in the '52 Game.
6. Rube Waddell, in 1901. He won 14 games for Chicago that season, left the team for the upstart American League and won 150 games over the next nine seasons.
7. Rick and Paul Reuschel in a 1975 Cubs game.
8. Hippo Vaughn in 1918 and Grover Cleveland Alexander in '20.
9. Ken Holtzman.
10. The Cubs signed Robin Roberts and traded for Ferguson Jenkins.
11. Ryan Dempster.
12. Willie Hernandez.
13. Jim Bullinger, who won 27 games with the Cubs over five years (and hit two more HRs).
14. Ken Holtzman.
15. Burt Hooten and Milt Pappas.
16. Rick James, who was 0-1 with a 13.50 ERA in his Big League career. The Cubs did select Ken Holtzman in the fourth round that year.
17. Ernie Broglio and Bobby Shantz.
18. Bob Buhl was 0-for-70 that season, and the following year snapped a MLB record 0-for-88 streak. He did win 12 games for the Cubs in 1962.
19. He had badly mangled fingers from sticking his hand into a corn chopper as a seven-year-old.
20. Hippo Vaughn on May 2, 1917. He gave up a hit and run in the 10th inning while the Cincinnati Reds' Fred Toney kept his no-hitter intact in the 10th.
21. Dennis Eckersley.
22. Bruce Sutter (in 1979) and Randy Myers (1993).
23. Bill Bonham on July 31, 1974. Kerry Wood struck out four in one inning in a 2002 game.
24. Kerry Wood.
25. Mike Morgan.

Pitcher's Round (from page 42)

1. Bruce SUTTER; 2. David PATTON; 3. Mitch ATKINS; 4. Don LARSEN; 5. Frank DIPINO; 6. Blaise ILSLEY; 7. Joe NIEKRO; 8. Jose GUZMAN. Mystery Name: Albert SPALDING. (Following his playing career, he founded the Spalding Sporting Goods Co. which supplied baseballs for the Major Leagues for more than 100 years.)

Pitchers' Crossword (from page 44)

CHAPTER 4

Cryptic Quote (from page 48)

"THE CHICAGO CUBS ARE LIKE RUSH STREET—A LOT OF SINGLES, BUT NO ACTION."

— JOE GARAGIOLA

Next-Door Neighbor (from page 48)

1. SOTO; 2. HUNDLEY; 3. DAVIS; 4. WILKINS; 5. GIRARDI; 6. SERVAIS; 7. SWISHER; 8. HARTNETT.

Catchers' Mini-Crossword (from page 49)

Additional Clue: FOOTE

Name Grid (from page 50)

```
    B M S             F D       B
    E C W I L S O N   O A       A
    R V I             O L       R
B U R G E S S         T A Y L O R     E
    Y Y H A R B I D G E               E
    H   E                   C H I T I
    I   B R E S N A H A N               T
    L   E                   E     C
M I L L E R               S E R V A I S
C     T H A C K E R ▓ M       N ▓ O
C   F E               H A R T N E T T
U   L L           K   N       I     O
L W I L L I A M S         I       Z
L   N             A   T       Z       W
O A T W E L L     N   T   G I R A R D I     I
U   H             T   R       R             L
G K L I N G   L I V I N G S T O N           K
H   T             A   D       O             I
S C H E F F I N G     G       D             N
          O W E N         D A V I S
```

Catchers' Crossword (from page 52)

Su-Gas-Ku (from page 57)

I	G	E	S	A	L	T	F	D
S	L	D	T	F	G	A	I	E
T	A	F	I	E	D	S	G	L
E	T	G	F	D	I	L	A	S
A	S	D	L	G	E	I	T	F
F	L	I	A	S	T	D	E	G
D	F	T	G	I	S	E	L	A
L	E	A	D	T	F	G	S	I
G	I	S	E	L	A	F	D	T

Catchers' Trivia (from page 54)

1. Rick Wilkins, who hit .303 with 30 home runs.
2. Hundley caught 160 games, including 147 complete games. Others who caught for the Cubs that season were Randy Bobb (7 appearances), John Boccabella (4), John Felske (3), Gene Oliver (1) and Bill Plummer (1).
3. El Tappe.
4. Joe Garagiola.
5. Cuno Barragan, who played just 69 games in his three-year career.
6. Michael Barrett.
7. Geovany Soto. He hit .341 with five home runs and 20 RBI that month.
8. The U.S. He was born and raised in San Juan, Puerto Rico, a U.S. territory.
9. Steve Swisher, who played four seasons with the Cubs.
10. Tyler Houston, Sandy Martinez and Scott Servais.
11. Jason Kendall (who played for the Cubs in 2007), whose father was Fred Kendall (who played for three teams from 1969-80).
12. Gabby Hartnett.
13. Joe Girardi.
14. Geovany Soto.
15. Henry Blanco. "Blanco" is Spanish for "white."
16. Steve Swisher, whose son, Nick, played the last two seasons with the New York Yankees.
17. Pocket billiards. Kling ran a pool hall while sitting out the season.
18. Jody Davis in 1986.
19. Koyie Hill.
20. From the observation area at the top of the Washington Monument in the nation's capital.
21. Randy Hundley.
22. Todd Hundley, who claimed his gesture was directed at fans of the visiting team sitting behind the dugout.

23. Damian Miller, whose stats and tendencies are under the name "Chris Gill" in various union-approved baseball video games.
24. Randy Hundley.
25. Geovany Soto.

CHAPTER 5

Chicago Cubes (from page 60)

1. A; 2. AT; 3. SAT; 4. CAST; 5. COATS; 6. CASTRO.

Double Play (from page 60)

1B BUCKNER, LEE; 2B BAKER, SANDBERG; 3B RAMIREZ, CEY; SS DUNSTON, THERIOT; 1B DURHAM, GRACE; 2B BECKERT, TRILLO; 3B SANTO, MADLOCK; SS KESSINGER, BANKS.

Across and Down Words (from page 61)

Across: BALL, BASE, FOUL, MITT, GAME, BUNT; Down: DOUBLE, HITTER, UMPIRE, SINGLE; Phrase: CUBS THIRD BASEMAN RON SANTO.

All Mixed Up (from page 62)

1. CAVARRETTA; 2. HERMAN; 3. HORNSBY; 4. TINKER; 5. EVERS; 6. CHANCE; 7. GONZALEZ; 8. BUECHELLE; 9. THORNTON; 10. DEJESUS.

Su-Bon-Kura (from page 62)

U	O	B	N	A	R
R	N	A	O	U	B
A	R	N	U	B	O
B	U	O	R	N	A
N	A	R	B	O	U
O	B	U	A	R	N

Infielders' Mini-Crossword (from page 67)

Additional Clue: SANTO

C	E	Y				L	E	A
O	V	A		T	H	U	M	P
P	E	W		H	A	B	I	T
	S	N	E	E	Z	E	R	
		A	R	E				
	E	P	S	I	L	O	N	
E	R	A	T	O		R	O	W
A	N	G	S	T		A	T	E
T	E	E				L	E	E

Infielders' Trivia (from page 63)

1. Gary Scott, who had only 175 career at bats in two Big League seasons, hitting .160.
2. Mark Bellhorn.
3. Ken Hubbs.

4. Ernie Banks.
5. Infielder Gene Baker, who was called up Aug. 31, 1953. However, Ernie Banks was the first African-American to play in a game for the Cubs, on Sept. 17, 1953.
6. Shawon Dunston.
7. Derrek Lee.
8. Roy Smalley, Jr. His son, Roy III, played for five American League teams, including the White Sox.
9. Jimmie Foxx.
10. Phil Cavaretta.
11. Jimmy Cooney on May 30, 1927. It was the last one in the NL until 1992.
12. Aramis Ramirez.
13. Heinie Zimmerman, who had led the NL in batting average and HR with the Cubs in 1912.
14. Ernie Banks (in 1960) and Don Kessinger (1969 and '70).
15. Eddie Waitkus, who was playing for the Philadelphia Phillies. He missed most the 1949 season because of his injuries, but was able to return to the Phillies' line-up in '50.
16. Steve Bilko (Sgt. Bilko) who played for the Cubs in 1954.
17. Vance Law, son of Vern Law.
18. Cliff Johnson. The game started May 28 and was suspended, due to darkness, with the score tied, 3-3, after 10 innings. It was resumed Aug. 8, and Johnson, who the Cubs had acquired in June, came off the bench for the winning hit.
19. Ryan Theriot and Mike Fontenot.
20. Ryne Sandberg.
21. Glenn Beckert.
22. Rogers Hornsby, who scored 156 runs in 1929.
23. Chuck Connors, who is best known for his starring role in *The Rifleman*. He played 66 games with the Cubs in 1951.
24. Joe Pepitone.
25. Carmen Fanzone.

Su-Wil-Ku (from page 66)

E	S	N	L	K	O	I	R	W
R	L	O	I	W	N	S	K	E
I	W	K	R	E	S	N	O	L
N	E	W	K	S	I	O	L	R
O	R	S	W	N	L	E	I	K
L	K	I	O	R	E	W	N	S
W	N	R	S	O	K	L	E	I
K	O	L	E	I	W	R	S	N
S	I	E	N	L	R	K	W	O

CHAPTER 6

Outfielders' Mini-Crossword (from page 70)

Additional Clue: HATCHER

Su-Daw-Son-Ku (from page 71)

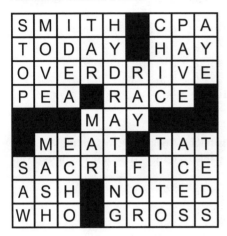

Double Switch (from page 71)

1. MOISES ALOU; 2. GARY MATTHEWS; 3. RICK MONDAY; 4. JOSE CARDENAL; 5. GEORGE ALTMAN; 6. HACK WILSON; 7. KIKI CUYLER; 8. LOU BROCK; 9. MARLON BYRD; 10. CHUCK KLEIN.

Cubs TXT (from page 72)

1. WILLIAMS; 2. DAWSON; 3. PHILLIPS; 4. SORIANO; 5. NADY; 6. PAFKO.

Outfielders, From A to Z (from page 73)

ALTMAN, BROWN, CRUZ, DAWSON, EDMONDS, FULD, GOODWIN, HICKMAN, IRVIN, JACKSON, KINGMAN, LAWTON, MARTINEZ, NORTH, O'LEARY, PATTERSON, QUALLS, RHODES, SMITH, THOMPSON, USHER, VARSHO, WOODS, FOX, YOUNG, ZAMBRANO.

Outfielders' Trivia (from page 76)

1. Billy Williams.
2. Peanuts Lowrey.
3. No one else has done it.
4. Ted Williams.
5. Frank "Wildfire" Schulte in 1911. Only four other players have accomplished that feat.
6. George H.W. Bush (41).
7. Gary Matthews.
8. Ralph Kiner, who hit 50 home runs in two seasons with the Cubs.
9. Glenallen Hill.

10. George Bell.
11. Jerome Walton, who followed his Rookie of the Year season with batting averages of .263, .219 and .127 before the Cubs released him.
12. Dwight Smith.
13. Rick Monday, who has the flag hanging on his living room wall.
14. Bobby Bonds, who played 45 games for the Cubs in 1981, his final Major League season. His son, Barry, hit a record 762 home runs.
15. Frank Ernaga, who despite his early success, hit just one other home run in his two-year, 29-game stint in the Big Leagues.
16. Andre Dawson.
17. Jerry Morales.
18. Rafael Palmeiro, who had 257 of those hits and 25 of the home runs, in his three seasons with the Cubs.
19. Alfonso Soriano.
20. Kosuke Fukudome, all with the Japanese national team.
21. Moises Alou.
22. Frank Demaree.
23. Billy Sunday.
24. Frank Secory, who played from 1944-46 with the Cubs.
25. Frankie Baumholtz, whose .290 career batting average was just below his .298 career field goal percentage.

Outfielders' Crossword (from page 74)

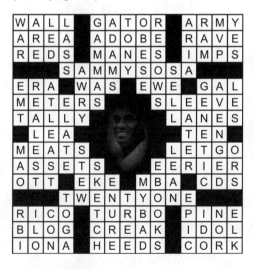

Su-Walt-Ku (from page 79)

A	L	M	W	N	T	O	R	Y
R	O	T	L	Y	A	N	M	W
W	N	Y	M	R	O	L	A	T
M	A	N	R	T	W	Y	L	O
T	Y	R	N	O	L	M	W	A
O	W	L	Y	A	M	R	T	N
Y	T	O	A	M	R	W	N	L
L	M	A	O	W	N	T	Y	R
N	R	W	T	L	Y	A	O	M

CHAPTER 7

Frey-ed (from page 82)

REYF, EYRF, YEFR.

Su-Pos-Ku (from page 82)

4	3	8	6	9	2	7	1	5
1	9	5	3	4	7	2	8	6
7	6	2	8	1	5	9	3	4
8	2	4	5	6	1	3	7	9
9	7	3	2	8	4	6	5	1
5	1	6	7	3	9	4	2	8
6	4	7	1	2	8	5	9	3
2	8	9	4	5	3	1	6	7
3	5	1	9	7	6	8	4	2

Managers' Mini-Crossword (from page 83)

Additional Clue: BOUDREAU

Q	U	A	D	E	■	L	A	C
U	N	S	A	Y	■	E	R	A
I	N	T	H	E	M	A	I	N
P	A	R	■	■	E	S	S	■
■	T	O	Y	■	D	E	T	■
■	U	T	E	■	■	B	O	P
F	R	U	S	T	R	A	T	E
O	A	R	■	U	N	C	L	E
E	L	F	■	B	A	K	E	R

Su-Do-Fri (from page 93)

F	I	R	S	H	C
S	H	C	F	I	R
C	R	H	I	S	F
I	S	F	C	R	H
R	F	I	H	C	S
H	C	S	R	F	I

Piniella Wordsmith (from page 84)

ALPINE, LIENAL, LINEAL, NIELLI, PENIAL, PINEAL, ALIEN, ALINE, ANILE, ELAIN, ILEAL, ILIAL, LAPEL, LAPIN, LIANE, LIPIN, PANEL, PENAL, PILEA, PILEI, PLAIN, PLANE, PLENA, ANIL, ELAN, ILEA, ILIA, INIA, LAIN, LANE, LEAL, LEAN, LEAP, LIEN, LINE, LIPA, LIPE, NAIL, NAPE, NEAP, NILL, NIPA, PAIL, PAIN, PALE, PALL, PANE, PEAL, PEAN, PEIN, PIAL, PIAN, PILE, PILI, PILL, PINA, PINE, PLAN, PLEA, PLIE.

Manage the Boxes (from page 85)

		H	A	C	K				
			C	H	A	N	C	E	
	P	I	N	I	E	L	L	A	
		M	C	C	A	R	T	H	Y
	E	L	I	A					
				G	R	I	M	M	
B	A	Y	L	O	R				
D	U	R	O	C	H	E	R		
L	O	F	T	U	S				
L	E	F	E	B	V	R	E		
	F	R	I	S	C	H			
	Z	I	M	M	E	R			
		S	P	A	L	D	I	N	G
	F	R	A	N	K	S			
		B	A	K	E	R			
	R	I	G	G	L	E	M	A	N
K	E	N	N	E	D	Y			
		F	R	E	Y				
	W	I	L	S	O	N			

Managers Word Search (from page 86)

Hidden Factoid: CAP ANSON IS THE WINNINGEST MANAGER IN CUBS HISTORY.

Managers' Crossword (from page 88)

```
F R E Y   E T U I   F L U F F
L U L U   F I N N   R A N E E
O P E C   T E S T   A D D I N
G E C K O     N O U N   E N D
S E T   M A M A   S K I R T
    E A G E R   E S T
M A R S H A L L     C E D E
P L A C A R D   M I S H E A R
H I G H     P I N I E L L A
    E B B   I R O N S
  D E W A R   M E N U   C H A
N O V   Y O K E     S W E A R
O R I E L   I N F O   A C N E
S I C K O   S T E W   L I O N
E S T E R   S O W N   E L I A
```

Managers' Trivia (from page 90)

1. Kansas City Royals, on Apr. 8, 1969.
2. First, in 2003.
3. Jim Essian. He won his first five games, but was fired at the end of the season with a 59-63 record.
4. Charlie Grimm.
5. Bob Kennedy.
6. Buck O'Neill.
7. Don Baylor, who was hired in 2000.
8. Lou Boudreau. Grimm was sent to the broadcast booth to replace Boudreau.
9. Jim Marshall.
10. Phil Cavaretta.
11. Joe McCarthy.
12. Rabbit Maranville.
13. All three had stints as the club's manager.
14. New York Yankees (1986-88), Cincinnati Reds (1990-92), Seattle Mariners (1993-2002) and Tampa Bay Devil Rays (2003-05).
15. Dusty Baker in 2003. He earned the honor by winning the NL pennant with the San Francisco Giants the previous season.
16. Washington Nationals.
17. Bruce Kimm.
18. Jim Lefebvre.
19. Don Zimmer, who was hired by Frey as a Cubs coach, then manager.
20. Cubs manager Lee Elia, early in the 1983 season. Elia joined the 15 percent of the non-working world when he was fired Aug. 22, 1983.
21. Jim Lefebvre.
22. Leo Durocher.

23. Houston Astros, in 1972 (and '73). He also managed in Japan briefly in 1976.
24. Whitey Lockman.
25. Gene Michael.

CHAPTER 8

Go Figure (from page 97)

1. 90; 2. 14; 3. 66; 4. 2; 5. 20; 6. 5. The final answer is 4.

Ifs and Thens (from page 97)

1908, the last time the Cubs won a World Series title.

Su-Tewks-Ku (from page 96)

E	Y	W	S	R	K	B	T	U
B	T	S	W	U	E	Y	K	R
R	K	U	Y	B	T	E	W	S
U	E	B	T	Y	R	W	S	K
W	R	K	U	E	S	T	Y	B
Y	S	T	B	K	W	R	U	E
S	U	Y	E	T	B	K	R	W
K	W	E	R	S	Y	U	B	T
T	B	R	K	W	U	S	E	Y

Su-Ple-Ku (from page 96)

C	L	A	P	E	S
S	E	P	C	L	A
A	P	S	L	C	E
L	C	E	A	S	P
P	S	L	E	A	C
E	A	C	S	P	L

By the Numbers Mini-Crossword (from page 99)

Additional Clue: JOHNSON

		O	N	E			
	S	H	O	E	I	N	G
	P	A	P	E	R	E	R
T	A	G	S		E	W	E	S
E	R	G			L	E	I
N	I	L	S		J	I	N	X
	N	E	P	T	U	N	E
	G	R	O	A	N	E	R
		T	W	O			

Add It Up (from page 98)

4	3	8
9	5	1
2	7	6

By the Numbers Word Search (from page 100)

```
I  K  I  S  T  E  P  H  E  N  S  O  N  L  H
L  U  O  D  L  W  I  T  H  O  R  N  S  B  Y
W  S  M  A  I  L  L  I  W  S  R  H  B  D  V
A  H  K  C  A  H  G  M  B  K  E  G  N  F  O
L  A  K  E  L  L  Y  S  S  R  U  U  O  L  M
B  E  L  G  R  E  B  D  N  A  S  A  S  U  G
R  O  R  S  N  R  T  L  I  L  C  V  L  N  I
C  P  O  O  S  I  P  O  K  C  H  M  I  D  J
B  R  O  W  N  U  L  G  N  C  E  D  W  G  H
Z  C  T  K  U  G  O  R  E  H  L  S  I  R  E
H  S  E  N  R  A  B  A  J  A  A  J  E  E  P
A  R  K  I  V  M  N  N  P  N  X  M  P  N  P
N  O  M  N  R  Q  N  S  T  C  I  M  M  N  P
D  E  D  T  A  Y  L  O  R  E  L  Y  U  C  D
S  R  E  V  E  B  N  N  W  I  J  K  E  A  M
```

By the Numbers Trivia (from page 102)

1. a.	10. a.	19. a.
2. b.	11. b.	20. b.
3. a.	12. c.	21. b.
4. b.	13. a.	22. a.
5. c.	14. a.	23. a.
6. c.	15. c.	24. a and b.
7. a.	16. a.	25. b.
8. b.	17. c.	
9. b.	18. b.	

By the Numbers Crossword (from page 106)

```
A D I E U   R O O T   S P A M
B A N K S   O P U S   A R E A
E M C E E   W I S P   L O R D
A M I D   C A N T   F E R A L
M I T   A O N E   T O M A T O
  N E W L Y   B O G   T E C
  G R I T   K A R L   T A S K
    C O I N C I D E S
J A C K   R I T E   C A M S
E R A   T A T   S H R E W
N A S D A Q   T R I O   L A P
K L E I N   W R A P   F I L E
I S L E   H I E S   L I S L E
N E A T   I N S T   A N S O N
S A W S   S O S A   G N A W S
```

CHAPTER 9

Wrigley Categories (from page 110)

Baseball Terms: WALK, RUN, INNING, GAME, LINE-UP, ERROR, YANKEE STADIUM; Cubs Pitchers: Kerry WOOD, Rick REUSCHEL, Blaise ILSLEY, John GAUB, Ted LILLY, Dennis ECKERSLEY, Anthony YOUNG; Cubs Outfielders: Jerome WALTON, Karl RHODES, Monte IRVIN, Joey GATHRIGHT, Don LANDRUM, Jim EDMONDS, Don YOUNG; Chicago Streets: WACKER Drive, RACINE Avenue, ILLINOIS Avenue, GRACE Avenue, LAKE SHORE Drive, EUCLID Avenue, YALE Avenue.

One and Only (from page 111)

Wrigley Field Crossword (from page 112)

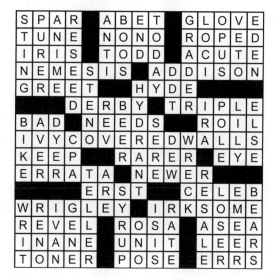

Word Cub-e (from page 114)

CINEOLE, CINEOL, ICONES, INCONY, RIDLEY, CINES, CIONS, CONES, CONNS, DONNE, DRILY, ELOIN, FENNY, FLOES, ICONS, NEONS, NICOL, NONES, NYLON, OLDIE, RILEY, YIELD, CINE, CION, COIN, COLD, COLE, COLY, CONE, CONI, CONN, CONS, CONY, DIEL, DIRL, DOES, DOLE, DONE, DONS, ENOL, EONS, EYNE, FEND, FENS, FEOD, FLEY, FLOC, FLOE, ICON, IDLE, IDLY, IDOL, INNS, IONS, LIDO, LOCI, LOIN, LONE, NEON, NODI, NOES, NONE, ONES, ONLY, RIEL, RILE, SEND, SNYE, YELD, YIRD, COD, COL, CON, DIE, DOC, DOE, DOL, DON, EFS, ELD, ELF, END, ENS, EON, FEN, FLY, INN, ION, LEI, LEY, LID, LIE, LYE, NOD, OES, OLD, OLE, ONE, ONS, RID, SEN, YID.

Wrigley Field Mini-Crossword (from page 115)

Additional Clue: BECKERT

A	T	E				S	E	T
C	O	M	B			S	H	A	H
T	R	U	E			E	A	S	E
			D	O	N	K	E	Y
S	H	E	F	F	I	E	L	D
T	O	M	A	T	O			
E	B	B	S			R	A	N	K
A	B	E	T			S	L	O	E
L	S	D				E	R	G

Su-Wain-Ku (from page 119)

E	S	I	H	N	A	W	U	O
H	O	A	S	W	U	E	I	N
N	W	U	I	E	O	S	H	A
O	U	E	A	H	S	N	W	I
A	H	W	N	O	I	U	S	E
S	I	N	W	U	E	A	O	H
W	A	O	U	I	N	H	E	S
I	N	H	E	S	W	O	A	U
U	E	S	O	A	H	I	N	W

Wrigley Field Trivia (from page 116)

1. Dave Kingman.
2. 11, six by the Cubs (including three by Dave Kingman).
3. Billy Sianis, who placed a hex on the team to never get to the World Series again. The goat was named Sonovia.
4. Harry Grossman, who said, "One, two, three...let there be lights!"
5. In 1943. The All-American Girls Professional Baseball League played games at Wrigley Field with temporary lighting.
6. An organ.
7. True, in 1937. Prior to that, bats were left on the ground, in foul territory, in front of the dugouts.
8. True, but it wasn't Chicago's Wrigley Field. It was Wrigley Field in Los Angeles, opened in 1925 and home to William Wrigley's Los Angeles Angels of the Pacific Coast League. The stadium was dismantled in 1966.
9. 1932. Charlie Root was the Cubs' pitcher.
10. Pete Rose of the Cincinnati Reds.
11. Marla Collins.
12. Yes, on May 18, 1967, more than 5,000 square feet of Astroturf was installed to cover the center field bleachers to help the batters' background. It was removed in 1982.
13. Pat Pieper.
14. Yosh Kawano.
15. Under Armour.
16. Eamus Catuli is Latin for Go Cubs! (However, there is no Latin word for Cubs. Catuli literally means "young animals."), and AC is short for Anno Catuli (Year of the "Cubs"), followed by the number of seasons since the Cubs won a division title (01 in 2010), a National League pennant (64 in 2010) and a World Series (101 in 2010).
17. Joe Mantegna.
18. 1990. Wrigley Field was also the site for the 1947 and '62 midseason classics.
19. The white flag has a blue W.
20. Gale Sayers.
21. Jimmy Buffett.
22. Ernie Banks.
23. Ryne Sandberg.
24. Northwestern University and the University of Illinois.
25. The Red Line.

CHAPTER 10

Missing Cubs (from page 122)

1. BUCKETS; 2. BECAUSE; 3. ABDUCTS; 4. BACKUPS; 5. BISCUIT; 6. BOUNCES; 7. BUNCHES; 8. COMBUST; 9. OBSCURE; 10. SUBJECT.

Su-Val-Ku (from page 122)

S	D	A	V	L	E
V	L	E	D	A	S
A	S	L	E	V	D
D	E	V	A	S	L
E	V	S	L	D	A
L	A	D	S	E	V

Extra Innings Mini-Crossword (from page 126)

Additional Clue: PEREZ

H	A	R	R	Y		F	B	I
E	N	N	U	I		E	L	M
S	T	A	M	P		L	I	P
		P	S	A	L	M		
	O	W	L		Z	A	P	
	T	H	E	T	A			
P	T	A		A	L	O	O	F
E	E	L		L	E	A	V	E
A	R	E		C	A	R	A	Y

Bare Bones Crosswords (from pages 123-124)

#1

#2

#3

#4

Word Transformations (from page 125)

WALK-BALK-BANK-BUNK-BUNT; BASE-BASS-BATS-OATS-OUTS; HITS-HATS-HATE-GATE-GAME; SLID-SLIM-SLAM-SEAM-TEAM; BELT-BENT-BUNT-RUNT-RUNS; CUBS-CUPS-COPS-COPE-HOPE.

Destined to be a Cub (from page 130)

1. RICHIE ASHBURN; 2. HEATHCLIFF SLOCUMB; 3. BARNEY SCHULTZ; 4. STEVE BUECHELE; 5. SCOTT BULLETT; 6. BRUCE SUTTER; 7. BILL SCHUSTER; 8. BRUCE EDWARDS; 9. TUCK STAINBACK; 10. BUCK COATS.

Su-Do-Bol (from page 131)

O	E	J	B	M	L	G	I	R
I	R	L	J	G	E	O	B	M
B	M	G	I	O	R	L	E	J
L	O	I	R	E	M	B	J	G
E	G	B	L	J	I	M	R	O
M	J	R	G	B	O	E	L	I
R	L	O	M	I	B	J	G	E
J	I	E	O	L	G	R	M	B
G	B	M	E	R	J	I	O	L

Extra Innings Crossword (from page 132)

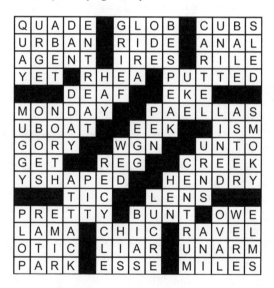

Q	U	A	D	E		G	L	O	B		C	U	B	S
U	R	B	A	N		R	I	D	E		A	N	A	L
A	G	E	N	T		I	R	E	S		R	I	L	E
Y	E	T		R	H	E	A		P	U	T	T	E	D
		D	E	A	F			E	K	E				
M	O	N	D	A	Y		P	A	E	L	L	A	S	
U	B	O	A	T		E	E	K		I	S	M		
G	O	R	Y		W	G	N		U	N	T	O		
G	E	T		R	E	G		C	R	E	E	K		
Y	S	H	A	P	E	D		H	E	N	D	R	Y	
	T	I	C		L	E	N	S						
P	R	E	T	T	Y	B	U	N	T		O	W	E	
L	A	M	A		C	H	I	C		R	A	V	E	L
O	T	I	C		L	I	A	R		U	N	A	R	M
P	A	R	K		E	S	S	E		M	I	L	E	S

Extra Innings Trivia (from page 127)

1. Harry's widow, Dutchie.
2. Jim Thorpe and Greasy Neale played for the Reds and Paddy Driscoll played for the Cubs.
3. Robin Jennings, whose father was in the foreign service.
4. Randy Myers.
5. Michael Jordan.
6. Danny and Hal Breeden.
7. Harry was an announcer with the Chicago White Sox.
8. He was a National Football League quarterback.
9. Dickie Noles. He was traded to the Detroit Tigers on Sept. 22 for a "player to be named later." On Oct. 23, the Tigers returned him to the Cubs as the "player to be named later."
10. Ron Santo in 1966, to protect a broken cheekbone.
11. HoHoKam Park.
12. Pinstripes.
13. True, but the vests were sent to the storage closet after the 1942 season.
14. True. The balls were tested during several games, but the results were mixed, so the yellow balls were nixed.
15. WMAQ.
16. Yes, in 1916, the Cubs had "Joa," a bear cub, living in a cage just outside the stadium.
17. Franklin Adams of the New York Evening Mail who wrote the poem "Baseball's Sad Lexicon" in 1910.
18. University of Illinois Medical Center.
19. Boise Hawks-A, Daytona Cubs-A, Dominican Cubs-Rookie, Iowa Cubs-AAA, Mesa Cubs-Rookie, Peoria Chiefs-A, Tennessee Smokies-AA.
20. Dan McGinn, who was 0-5 with a 5.89 ERA in his only season with the Cubs.
21. Jeff Samardzija. The great Cap Anson spent two years at Notre Dame's boarding school for young students.
22. Jack Brickhouse, a Cubs announcer from 1948-81.
23. The Cubs and New York Mets played two games in Tokyo, Japan, to start the season. Those were the first Major League regular season games played outside of North America.
24. The winning Dodgers had Burt Hooten and Rick Monday. The Yankees had Barry Foote, Oscar Gamble, Dave LaRoche, Bobby Murcer and Rick Reuschel.
25. Hayden Simpson, a right handed pitcher from Southern Arkansas.